QUALITY AT WORK

A Personal Guide to Professional Standards

Diana Bonet and Rick Griggs

A FIFTY-MINUTE™ SERIES BOOK

QUALITY AT WORK
A Personal Guide to Professional Standards

Diana Bonet
Rick Griggs

CREDITS
Editor: **Michael G. Crisp and Elaine Fritz**
Designer: **Carol Harris**
Typesetting: **Interface Studio**
Cover Design: **Amy Shayne and Fifth Street Design**
Artwork: **Ralph Mapson**

© 1989 by Crisp Publications, Inc.
Printed in the United States of America by Von Hoffmann Graphics, Inc.

CrispLearning.com

02 03 04   10 9 8 7 6 5 4

Library of Congress Catalog Card Number 88-72262
Bonet, Diana and Griggs, Rick
Quality At Work
ISBN 0-931961-72-6

LEARNING OBJECTIVES FOR:

QUALITY AT WORK

The objectives for *Quality at Work* are listed below. They have been
developed to guide you, the reader, to the core issues covered
in this book.

Objectives

- ❑ 1) **To show how professional quality standards benefit organizations**

- ❑ 2) **To show how to implement quality at work**

- ❑ 3) **To explain potential problems in achieving quality at work**

Assessing Your Progress

In addition to the learning objectives, Crisp Learning has developed
an **assessment** that covers the fundamental information presented
in this book. A 25-item, multiple-choice and true-false questionnaire
allows the reader to evaluate his or her comprehension of the
subject matter. To learn how to obtain a copy of this assessment,
please call **1-800-442-7477** and ask to speak with a Customer Service
Representative.

Assessments should not be used in any employee selection process.

ABOUT THE AUTHORS

Diana Bonet develops and conducts seminars on listening, speaking and writing for major corporations throughout the United States, Canada and Europe. Author of more than five great-selling Crisp books, Diane is also an active member of the International Listening Association and the National Speaker's Association.

Rick Griggs is an experienced trainer, speaker, consultant, and author. In 1993 he founded Griggs Achievement to research and present achievement principles and personal life balance. In addition, he started Manfit Press (a division of Griggs Achievement) to offer vital books on management and career success.

He has consulted for many US public and private organizations and has written or co-written five books covering quality, balance, optimism and loyalty.

PREFACE

Quality is a standard by which we judge our work. It measures whether we did what we set out to do and is the standard by which customers measure products or services. To establish quality guidelines, we must have a starting point and some no-nonsense criteria. A quality program must also be fun and rewarding to get enthusiastic support. QUALITY AT WORK makes a breakthrough by presenting the basics of quality in an easy-to-understand format designed to help management and employees establish and meet simple, effective quality standards.

This book is for everyone who works. As an employee, you make a significant contribution to your organization by bringing high personal standards to your job. This book helps you examine the role of quality in your life and work.

If you are a supervisor or manager, you will find step-by-step guidance and a clear definition of quality. You alone provide the leadership and support needed for a strong quality program. QUALITY AT WORK helps you and your colleagues set realistic standards for departmental and organizational goals.

QUALITY AT WORK is about personal and job-related quality. Sections 1–3 help the reader identify the personal quality standards and goals that support their quality standards at work. Sections 4–7 relate more closely to work issues.

Section 1 defines quality, provides examples of quality, and tells why it is important. Quality begins with the individual, and in **Section 2** you have the opportunity to assess your individual standards of quality. How were they developed? Why are they important? How do they relate to your work? **Section 3** discusses the intangibles of quality—commitment, competence, and communication. In order to establish quality standards we must know the purpose of our individual jobs and the work of our organization.

Section 4 identifies organizational goals and gives guidelines for setting quality goals based on our work purpose. In **Section 5** you will find a Seven-Step Plan that you and your department can use to establish Perfection Standards (P.S.) to determine what quality work is. (What is quality for one job or service may not be quality for another. An industrial diamond does not have to be as nearly perfect as one that will be used as a setting in fine jewelry. Quality depends on purpose.)

Section 6, the "How-To" chapter, provides valuable guidelines on quality issues, including problem solving, customer satisfaction, measuring results, rewarding quality performance, setting up quality groups, providing training, assessing the cost of quality, establishing a quality program, and supporting your quality program. **Section 7** discusses error prevention and supports the concept of doing the job right the first time.

This book is for people concerned about quality. Of course no one is against quality, but implementing personal and work-related guidelines can be frustrating. QUALITY AT WORK answers the question: How can we set quality standards that are personally satisfying and help our organization do what we say we will do when we say we will do it, in a way that meets our customers' needs?

If quality is your goal, we can help. We hope you enjoy using our material. Turn the page and let's get started.

Diana Bonet

Rick Griggs

CONTENTS

ACKNOWLEDGMENTS

We wish to thank the following people for their valuable contributions to this book. Their support has added depth and breadth to the content of the book and enriched our lives. These individuals have proved by example that quality at work, works!

John Asquith—Student Researcher, Stanford University

Catherine Ayers—Director, Office of Business, Industry & Government, De Anza College, Cupertino, CA

Dave Burgett—Project Engineer, Teledyne McCormick Selph, Hollister, CA

Ed Diehl—Corporate Quality Manager, Triad Systems Corporation, Livermore, CA

Rick Gilbert—President, Frederick Gilbert & Assoc., Redwood City, CA

Patricia Goelzer—Manager, Plan Administration and Retirement Services, Weyerhaeuser Company, Tacoma, WA

Richard Gordon—Director, Career Builders, Ltd., Brisbane, Australia

Jon Green—Director of Quality, Pacific Bell, San Ramon, CA

Walt Hurd—Chairman, Harrington, Hurd & Squires, Los Gatos, CA

Patricia Lowell—President, Plaza Bank of Commerce, San Jose, CA

Wendy Coleman Lucas—Assistant Editor, Levi Strauss, Quality Enhancement Administrator, San Francisco, CA

Joe Shea—Vice President, Triad Systems Corporation, Livermore, CA

Terry Stamps—Training Manager, Hewlett-Packard Corporation, Sunnyvale, CA

Greg Swartz—President, Swartz & Associates, Mountain View, CA

A special thanks to Tom and Louise Clifton, parents of Diane Bone, for their ongoing examples of high personal standards.

SE**CT**I**O**N
I

QUALITY CONSCIOUSNESS

> *There is no limit to the quality that can be produced, even in the most menial job.*
>
> Dave Thomas

Quality is a standard, a goal, or a set of requirements. Quality is a measurable goal, not a vague sense of goodness. It is a continual effort to improve rather than a set degree of excellence. It is a result. We cannot possess quality, we can only practice it. *Quality is a perfection standard by which we decide whether we did what we set out to do when and how we said we would do it, in a way that meets our customers' needs.* Were our customers happy with the way we provided our service or made our widgets? If so, we can say we met our quality goals.

Dr. J. M. Juran says that manufacturing quality is "fitness for purpose." In service industries which are somewhat subjective, we say that a quality service is one that is "fit to be tried." In other words, employees have agreed to try quality practices and measure quality results through customer feedback. An A+ report card from internal and external customers is the final test of quality.

*NOTE: For definitions of additional commonly used quality terms, see the glossary on page 85.

QUALITY CONSCIOUSNESS CHECKLIST

Quality begins with awareness. You probably developed an early ''quality consciousness'' as a consumer. Remember how you liked the mint-green toothpaste better than the white kind? Later you made many life choices based on quality: where you lived and worked, who your friends were, what lifestyle you wanted. Consider each of the following statements and mark it true or false based on your current awareness of quality at work and in your personal life. See the authors' comments on the next page.

True/False

_T_   1. Quality is preventing problems rather than picking up the pieces afterward.

_T_   2. Quality can always be improved.

_T_   3. The KISS (Keep It Simple, Stupid!) method is the best way to insure quality.

_T_   4. The most important reason for a quality program at work is to have satisfied customers.

_F_   5. Constant attention to quality is unnecessary.

_F_   6. First impressions aren't important in creating a quality environment.

_T_   7. Quality is the little things as well as the big things.

_T_   8. A quality program must have management support to be successful.

_F_   9. Quality guidelines are best communicated by word-of-mouth.

_T_   10. Most people want to do quality work.

CHECKLIST (CONTINUED)

True/False

F   11. Customers pay little attention to quality.

T   12. A quality program must mesh with the organization's goals and profit plans.

T   13. Quality means conformance to standards.

T   14. Quality should operate in all parts of a business.

F   15. Personal quality standards and business quality standards have little in common.

T   16. Quality requires commitment.

T   17. Quality relates to the process as much as to the goal.

F   18. People who talk about quality are idealists.

ANSWERS: 1.–4. T; 5. F (Quality does not take care of itself. It takes time, energy, and creativity to maintain a successful quality program.) **6. F** (The first impression may be the only chance to sell an idea, service, or product. Quality is important down to the smallest detail, and it has to be right—the first time.) **7. T, 8. T, 9. F** (Quality guidelines must be issued officially from the top and they must be in writing. They should also be agreed to by employees.) **10. T, 11. F** (Customers today are sophisticated and demanding, and pay as much attention to quality as to price.) **12.–14. T, 15. F** (Personal and business quality standards are inseparable. People with high personal standards will be the ones to lead business quality programs.) **16.–17. T, 18. F** (People who talk about quality are realists. The only way to compete successfully today is to continually improve quality.)

WHERE THERE'S SMOKE...

Imagine what would happen if an emergency service neglected to attend to issues of quality. The following scene illustrates how much we are dependent on professionals in the public sector to make quality a high priority.

The warning bell in the Fourth Street Fire Hall sounds abrasively as Patrick shakes himself awake. It is 3:00 a.m. and a two-alarm fire is burning out of control in a vacant warehouse a mile away. The on-duty fire crew slowly pull themselves from their warm cots and fumble for their coats and boots. "Where are my gloves?" wonders Patrick as he saunters toward Engine #1. Recently he noticed that the old truck had been given to spells of battery failure. "Should report that," thought Patrick idly.

Patrick gives a final wrap to secure a water hose on the truck. A loose nozzle falls from the attached hose and clatters to the floor. "Should fix that," he mutters, as he climbs into the cab and yells for everyone to climb aboard. The crew grumbles as it climbs on the tail board. Joe, the rookie, is nowhere to be seen.

"Hey, Joe, let's go!" yells Patrick. Joe appears, looking sleepy and confused. "I thought this was another false alarm," he says.

"Get on, Joe, this is the real thing," yells Patrick, slightly annoyed. Patrick cranks the key on the big red engine and the engine grinds hesitantly, then dies. "Should get this fixed," Patrick growls. "Okay, everyone, battery trouble. Unload and reload on Engine #2."

Engine #2 swings slowly from the firehouse. Joe hangs precariously from the safety bar scratching his head. "I sure thought this was a false alarm."

ANALYZE THE EXAMPLE

If this story had been true, what were the crew's chances of getting to the fire before the building was destroyed? In your opinion, what quality problems did the Fourth Street Company have? Check your responses from the list below.

☐   No clear guidelines for quality standards

☐   Poor maintenance

☐   Poor team spirit

☐   Inadequate training

☐   No sense of urgency

☐   Lack of communication

☐   Unconcerned leadership

☐   No preventive thinking

Others _____

If you checked all of them, you're right! Fortunately, the Fourth Street Company doesn't exist. However, their problems *do* exist in many businesses because they are not yet quality conscious. They need to understand quality and why it is important to adopt a quality program.

THE "NO WORSE" TRAP

In *A Passion for Excellence,* * Tom Peters tells this startling story:

> Quality is about passion and pride. Sometime back Tom spent two days in a series of seminars with managers of a major retail chain. In the course of the meeting the subject of affordable levels of service came up continually. At one point Tom was well launched on a bit of a diatribe about the rotten level of service in retailing in general when an executive vice president, in front of forty of his peers and subordinates, got up and interrupted him: "Tom, sit down and calm down. Or get off our case. It's a changing and complex and highly competitive world. *We are no worse than anybody else.*"

To avoid the "No Worse" trap, individuals and organizations need to look realistically at quality. It is not an impossible dream; it is an everyday reality practiced by thousands of people and organizations that see the payoff for setting standards and living up to them.

---

*A Passion For Excellence, Tom Peters, 1985 Random House, New York

WHAT QUALITY IS AND IS NOT

Here is a list of attributes describing what quality is and is not. Use this list to identify your personal and professional responses to the quality challenge. Add your own ideas at the bottom.

QUALITY IS:	QUALITY IS NOT:
A philosphy	A quick fix
Conformance to perfection standards	Goodness
Prevention	Merely inspection
Following specific guidelines	A "close enough" attitude
A lifelong process	A motivational program
Commitment	Coincidence
Supported by upper management	Randomly adopted
A positive attitude	A watchdog mentality
Agreement	Do your own thing
Willing communication	Isolated data
Understanding your processes	Guessing
Identifying opportunities for error	Detecting errors in end products
Add your own:	Add your own:
_____	_____
_____	_____
_____	_____

QUALITY AT WORK

Quality At Work

WHY WORRY ABOUT QUALITY?

Why should our organization develop a quality consciousness? Why should we adopt a quality program? What are the advantages of moving from a random method of ''putting out fires'' to a preventive, planned system for delivering quality goods and services? List as many reasons as you can think of in the space below. Place a ☑ next to those that are most important to you. Then turn the page and read ''Twenty Reasons to Adopt a Quality Program.'' Check any you would like to add to your list.

REASONS TO ADOPT A QUALITY PROGRAM

Important
To Me

☐ _____

☐ _____

☐ _____

☐ _____

☐ _____

☐ _____

☐ _____

WHAT, ME WORRY?

TWENTY REASONS TO ADOPT A QUALITY PROGRAM

Important
To Me

☐ 1. To be profitable

☐ 2. To be "recession proof"

☐ 3. To enjoy the results

☐ 4. To reinforce personal quality standards

☐ 5. To maintain customer confidence

☐ 6. To build customer loyalty

☐ 7. To improve customer satisfaction

☐ 8. To maintain corporate vitality

☐ 9. To use employees' creative energies

☐ 10. To develop a good reputation

☐ 11. To promote human dignity

☐ 12. To lower costs

☐ 13. To retain employees

☐ 14. To increase productivity

☐ 15. To contribute to society

☐ 16. To create a clear vision of the organization

☐ 17. To improve technology

☐ 18. To solve problems effectively

☐ 19. To increase competitiveness

☐ 20. To develop internal cooperation

Add your own:

☐ _____

☐ _____

☐ _____

THE CHALLENGE OF QUALITY

Quality is an elusive goal. Once you have produced a quality product or service, you must sustain and improve that level. Quality is a moving target. Your competition improves, customers evolve and demand changes, and supplies become scarce. Check the suggestions that you think will help you meet your personal and professional quality goals.

☐ Learn all you can about quality.

☐ Apply quality standards to appropriate work issues.

☐ Blame others when quality wavers.

☐ Work with others in accomplishing your quality goals.

☐ Don't worry about a little inconsistency.

☐ Know how your quality goals relate to your organization's mission.

List below some quality challenges in your work or your personal life and list one or two solutions that will help you meet them.

Challenge	Solution(s)
1. _____	_____
	_____
2. _____	_____
	_____
3. _____	_____
	_____
4. _____	_____
	_____
5. _____	_____
	_____

PERSONAL QUALITY STANDARDS

> *Quality involves living the message of the possibility of perfection and infinite improvement, living it day in and day out, decade by decade.*
>
> Tom Peters

Your personal quality standards are what make you say, ''Wow, that waitress is doing a great job!'' These same standards cause you to think, ''If I get service this lousy again at the counter, I'll never come back!''

Everywhere you drive, each time you buy your lunch, and every time you make a purchase, you are applying your personal standards of quality. We all make quick judgments about the workers on the side of the road: some do an excellent job, while others just sit. We tell our co-workers that the service at the new lunch deli is terrible, but the roast beef is delicious. And each time we buy stockings, shirts, shoes, or jewelry we evaluate the way we're treated by the sales clerk.

In all of these cases, we're using our personal standards for quality to assess whether other people are doing what they said they would do, when they said they would do it.

DEFINITION

Personal quality standards are the acid tests *we use on ourselves and others to see if we act and perform the way we said (or implied) we would act.*

Albert Einstein said that ''Whoever is careless with the truth in small matters cannot be trusted with important matters.'' This can be scary. At first glance, we might think that every little thing in our lives is extremely important and that every detail must be perfect. How can you keep track of everything and still do it to the highest level of performance? The answer is: *Pick your battles and then perform as agreed.*

PERSONAL QUALITY STANDARDS
(Continued)

See what you think of the following personal quality standards. Take a look at the subject or topic of the standard and also the *level of performance* attached to each one. Compare these standards with your own, and check whether yours are the same, higher or lower.

My standards are:

Higher	Same	Lower		
☐	☐	☐	1.	Get to all appointments within *5 minutes* of the agreed time.
☐	☐	☐	2.	*Never* criticize family members in front of outsiders.
☐	☐	☐	3.	Stay within *10 miles* of the speed limit.
☐	☐	☐	4.	*Never* speed in school zones or near children.
☐	☐	☐	5.	Exercise at least *twice a week*.
☐	☐	☐	6.	Wear *only* neat clean clothing outside of the house.
☐	☐	☐	7.	Write checks no more than *one day* before depositing the money.
☐	☐	☐	8.	Return phone calls within *one hour* of receiving the message.
☐	☐	☐	9.	Flirt *occasionally* with attractive men/women in *social situations*.

NOTICE YOUR PERSONAL STANDARDS

You may have noticed that some of these personal quality standards make you feel uncomfortable. You have already compared them to your own personal expectations *and* you've made a judgment call about whether they're too strict or too lenient.

If your personal standards are rather strict, you may have thought:

- Ten miles above the speed limit is illegal and I wouldn't do it.
- Exercising only twice a week isn't good enough for cardiovascular fitness.
- How could someone *think* of writing a check *before* depositing the money?
- You should never flirt!

If your personal standards do not focus on these areas, you may have thought:

- Heck, I go 20 miles above the speed limit. My radar detector helps!
- Exercising twice a month is more than enough. You could kill yourself!
- If a check bounces, they can send it through again...I'm not a crook!
- Romance is the spice of life! There's nothing wrong with it, even at work.

NOTICE YOUR STANDARDS

PREPARING TO DEVELOP PERSONAL STANDARDS

A. | LIST THE DIFFERENT AREAS OF YOUR LIFE. |

This may seem strange at first: name all the areas that are important to you in your personal life. Examples: Health, Family, Hobbies, Finances, Leisure, Travel, Growth, Relationships, Career, Education, Reading, and Writing.

_____ _____ _____ _____

_____ _____ _____ _____

_____ _____ _____ _____

B. | PRIORITIZE THE AREAS OF YOUR LIFE. |

Putting them in order will attach a priority to each segment of your personal life. You may choose to focus only on certain areas.

1st_____ 2nd_____ 3rd_____ 4th_____

5th_____ 6th_____ 7th_____ 8th_____

9th_____ 10th_____ 11th_____ 12th_____

C. | LIST THE GOAL OR END RESULT. |

Now imagine how your life will look when the top 4—5 priority areas are fully developed. Some of your personal areas will have values attached (for example, honesty, loyalty, trust). Examples of goals: 1st = Honest/open family communications. 2nd = Healthy/fit body. 3rd = New career paths.

	LIFE AREA	*END RESULT/GOAL*
1st	_____	_____
2nd	_____	_____
3rd	_____	_____
4th	_____	_____
5th	_____	_____

PREPARING TO DEVELOP PERSONAL STANDARDS (CONTINUED)

D. | DESCRIBE SPECIFIC ACTIVITIES TO REACH EACH GOAL. |

These are the steps you take to reach end results. In other words, list the means to the end. In cases where no specific end result is targeted, the process or the means is most important.

Remember: The goal is the *end result*, and the activities are what get you there.

Example: 1st Goal: *Receive my college degree.*

Activities: a. *Sign up for classes.* b. *Attend classes.* c. *Pass tests.*

1st Goal: _____

Activities: a. _____ b. _____ c. _____

2nd Goal: _____

Activities: a. _____ b. _____ c. _____

3rd Goal: _____

Activities: a. _____ b. _____ c. _____

4th Goal: _____

Activities: a. _____ b. _____ c. _____

5th Goal: _____

Activities: a. _____ b. _____ c. _____

MY PERSONAL STANDARDS

> *"I don't believe in setting up universal standards that a large proportion of people can't reach."*
>
> Margaret Mead

Write down your initial ideas for personal standards. Don't worry about whether they are perfectly thought out or well written. Just jot down some areas you feel are important and how strict you want to be in each area. *Base these standards on the goals and activities you listed as important to you in the last few pages. Ignore the P-A-S options column.* You'll fill it out later.

Examples: A. Never miss more than one class session per semester.
B. Receive at least average passing grades on all tests.

	P-A-S Options		
	P	A	S
1.	☐	☐	☐
2.	☐	☐	☐
3.	☐	☐	☐
4.	☐	☐	☐
5.	☐	☐	☐
6.	☐	☐	☐
7.	☐	☐	☐
8.	☐	☐	☐
9.	☐	☐	☐
10.	☐	☐	☐

You'll find that you actually do have standards in your personal life and an idea of how strictly you feel they should be observed.

Before discussing the level of quality for each standard, let's take a look at some examples of personal standards and a quick "acid test" for measuring quality. We'll come back to this page later.

IS THIS PERSONAL QUALITY?
YOU DECIDE!

James drives into a clean and apparently efficient gas station to fill up. As he drives in he sees a woman pull out, so he takes the same unleaded pump she had just used.

There's no one around, so he steps over a large puddle of water and starts pumping. When the tank is half full, an attendant casually walks up and says, "Hey, bud, you better be careful, that puddle you're standing in isn't water...it's gas. The hose broke on a lady a while ago...you should've seen the gas spurting out!"

James asks, "Well, why don't you clean it up? Customers don't expect to come here and step in gasoline!" The attendant replies, "Ah, it'll evaporate. That'll be $12.50 for your fill-up, sir."

What do you think about:

This attendant's personal standards: _____

Is quality an issue here? _____

What would your standard be? _____

IS THIS PERSONAL QUALITY?
YOU DECIDE! (CONTINUED)

Martin works in a high-rise building. His window used to overlook a park and an old office building. The office building was torn down to build the new City Hall and cultural complex. Martin is fascinated as he watches the daily progress. He is also surprised at some of the things the workers do right in front of his 12-story building, where dozens of people could be watching!

SCENE 1: Martin looks up from his computer and can't believe what he sees. There's a worker taking off his pants in broad daylight! He casually tosses them onto a truck and grabs his overalls. He then calmly slips into his overalls, totally unaware of 12 stories of office workers possibly watching him from across the street.

What do you think about:

This person's personal standards: _____

Is quality an issue here? _____

What would your standard be? _____

SCENE 2: A few weeks later, Martin sees that the underground parking level is complete, and workers are on the second story planning to lay concrete. One worker finishes a soft drink, looks around to see if other workers are looking, and then quickly throws the can between two walls of the new building. The can will probably never see light until an excavation team unearths the building in 2000 years.

What do you think about:

This person's personal standards: _____

Is quality an issue here? _____

What would your standard be? _____

IS THIS PERSONAL QUALITY?
YOU DECIDE! (CONTINUED)

At the Post Office

Here's a conversation that was overheard at the post office. Keep in mind that every large organization has a variety of people with different standards for quality. Sometimes other people's standards don't match our own or those of the organization. This does not mean they are good or bad.

This interchange was frustrating to the woman and the person who saw it take place. What do you think of the standards of quality involved?

Woman: *"Hi, I've driven over to pick up my package. What a long line!"*

Postal Employee: *"Do you have the yellow slip we put in your box?"*

Woman: *"I think so; let' see. . .Oh, here it is. . .I'm kind of in a rush!"*

Postal Employee: *"Wait here, I'll be right back." (several minutes pass.)*
"I'm sorry ma'am, we can't find it. Are you sure you didn't already pick it up?"

Woman: *"What? Of course not. I made a special trip down just for this package."*

Postal Employee: *"Well, I'll check again. . ." (several more minutes pass.)*
"Sorry, it's just not here. Are you sure. . .oh wait, what's your box number?"

Woman: *"It's number 1482."*

Postal Employee: *"Uh-oh, somebody put it in the wrong box; sorry!"*

Woman: *"Are you kidding! I wasted all this time?"*

Postal Employee: *"Hey, I just work here—I don't put the notes in the boxes."*

What do you think about:

This person's personal standards: _____

Is quality an issue here? _____

What would your standard be? _____

LIGHTING THE *QUALITY* *M-A-T-CH*

Is there a quick and useful way to compare what you do (and what others do) to some standard? We think there is, and believe it or not, it doesn't have to be complicated. Just remember the quality mnemonic: Q-MATCH which is:

```
QUALITY =
            M   EETS
            A   GREED
            T   ERMS &
            CH  ANGES
```

You could say that Q-MATCH is the light that illuminates the principle of quality. You can apply this acid test to yourself and the important things you do, or to others and the critical tasks they have agreed to perform. The terms and changes are not always plastered across an ad in the daily paper. In some cases, terms and changes are just implied, but quality is judged on implications as much as on written contracts.

When you're in these situations ask yourself if the service, performance, or activity really **M**eets **A**greed **T**erms and **CH**anges.

- At your bank
- At the drugstore
- Getting your shoes shined
- Purchasing a computer
- Service at a restaurant
- Getting the newspaper each day
- Repaying a loan
- Borrowing supplies from a co-worker
- Showing up for team practice

THE Q-MATCH TEST

The Acid Test: Does It Q-MATCH?: If it meets agreed-upon terms and changes, it's quality! Remember, although there are different levels of performance, the test is whether it matches what was agreed. Quality at the personal level can mean getting the boy or girl to deliver the paper anywhere on the lawn *or* specifically to the door mat. Both are quality if they are agreed on. You can also *change* the requirement by asking that they put the paper behind the fence so it won't get wet or stolen. This new change now defines the performance needed...in other words the level of quality. Take a look and see if these pass the test:

YES NO

☐ ☐   1.   Your auto mechanic takes two extra days to finish some repairs on your car. **Q-MATCH?**

☐ ☐   2.   The same mechanic lets you know in advance how long it will take and gives you a loaner car. **Q-MATCH?**

☐ ☐   3.   Your date or spouse cancels a weekly outing at the last minute. **Q-MATCH?**

☐ ☐   4.   Your scheduled appointment cancels *again* on the day of the scheduled meeting. **Q-MATCH?**

☐ ☐   5.   You feel a little ill and decide to skip an appointment and catch a movie instead. **Q-MATCH?**

☐ ☐   6.   While jogging, you decide to cut through the parking lot to save time and effort. **Q-MATCH?**

☐ ☐   7.   The rent or mortgage is due, but it's late Friday so you wait until Monday to pay. **Q-MATCH?**

☐ ☐   8.   You quit smoking, but continue to take puffs from friends' cigarettes; that way you're not really smoking. **Q-MATCH?**

☐ ☐   9.   Your doctor's appointment gets canceled. They called and left a message the day before. **Q-MATCH?**

☐ ☐   10.   A teenage boy agrees to clean and wash the car in order to use it tonight. His date changed to tomorrow night, but the car is still cleaned and washed today. **Q-MATCH?**

22

WHERE CAN I APPLY Q-MATCH?

Our quality test should be applied to any situation you feel is important. As you get used to using Q-MATCH, you'll find yourself assessing quality performance in an instant.

The Q-MATCH test can help you...

- Make purchase decisions
- Negotiate for repairs
- Weigh alternatives for investing
- Determine who to contact for social affairs
- Decide who to involve in business matters

In other words, anytime you deal with products, services, or activities where you expect certain levels of performance or satisfaction, use the Q-MATCH test to assess quality.

TAKE THE Q-MATCH TEST

QUALITY AND EXPECTATIONS

A lot of this business of quality boils down to agreed-upon expectations. It's very simple. One party makes a list of what they expect. This might be written, verbal, or even a mental note. Another party responds by giving details about which expectations they can and cannot meet. The two parties come to an agreement on what will be delivered and then the delivery is measured against the agreement.

1. Expectations (requirements)
2. Capabilities
3. Agreement (terms, promises, ads)
4. Delivery (performance)
5. Measurement

A STORY OF EXPECTATIONS

Rafael manages a department for a medium-sized, high technology firm. His group is responsible for shipping the finished products sold by the marketing department and built by manufacturing. In the past, Rafael tried to please everyone in marketing by promising early delivery dates with special last-minute requests. He also wanted to be on good terms with manufacturing, so he didn't complain when production schedules got bogged down and delivery dates were missed. Rafael learned the hard way that he couldn't meet everyone's expectations. Marketing, manufacturing, and even a few customers made formal complaints about the quality of his department. Today, Rafael has made it policy that everyone in the department follows the five steps mentioned above. They get detailed expectations and then match their capabilities. An agreement is reached to deliver only on the expectations they are capable of meeting. Finally, the performance delivery is measured against the written agreement. Rafael doesn't win all the popularity contests but he doesn't get dinged for poor quality either.

BEFORE THE FIVE STEP PROCESS

P-A-S OPTIONS FOR QUALITY

Quality is not perfection or goodness. Quality at work or at home is meeting expectations. Sometimes it means zero mistakes or defects, while at other times less-than-perfect performance still gives us what we require. Quality means that you **M**eet **A**greed **T**erms and **CH**anges.

P-A-S OPTIONS FOR QUALITY

PERFECTION Option: No mistakes, zero defects, inflexible

AVERAGE Option: Past results are fine, very flexible

STRETCH Option: Reasonable difficulty, little flexibility

Don't build the habit of failing. Set the right standard from the beginning. Average is appropriate for many situations. Others require the *stretch* or *perfection* options. *Pick the right one at the beginning and obtain an agreement.* This is quality.

Look at the standards you set earlier in the chapter. Go back to page 16 and add P-A-S options to identify which level of performance would be appropriate.

MEASURING PERSONAL STANDARDS

Measuring your personal goals and standards can only be done by you, because only by using your personal yardstick will you know if you're on the right track. You can measure according to subjective feelings (good or bad), reports from other important people, or your sense of satisfaction.

Personal quality standards are measured differently from your standards at work, because they result from your values, attitudes, and intuitive judgment. Work standards, on the other hand, must be quantifiable, observable, and results-oriented.

PERSONAL STANDARDS

- values
- attitudes
- intuitive judgment

WORK STANDARDS

- quantifiable
- observable
- results oriented

A BALANCED COMBINATION

The Personal Standard Measurement form on the facing page will help you quantify whether you are meeting your personal standards.

PERSONAL STANDARD MEASUREMENT FORM

Copy this page for each of your personal standards you listed on page 16. Then circle the number for the way you're currently performing to this standard. Not all measures will apply to each standard. Add any other measures that are important to you.

MY PERSONAL STANDARD #(   ) _____

---

1. SUBJECTIVE FEELINGS
Feels Wrong   Feels Right

| 1 | 2 | 3 | 4 | 5 |

2. DEGREE OF HAPPINESS
Extremely Unhappy   Extremely Happy

| 1 | 2 | 3 | 4 | 5 |

3. PERSONAL SATISFACTION
No Satisfaction   Complete Satisfaction

| 1 | 2 | 3 | 4 | 5 |

4. PERSONAL VALUES
Doesn't Match   Matches
My Values   My Values

| 1 | 2 | 3 | 4 | 5 |

5. INTUITIVE JUDGMENT
Something Tells Me   Something Tells Me
It's Wrong   It's Right

| 1 | 2 | 3 | 4 | 5 |

6. OUTSIDE FEEDBACK
Trusted Friends/   Trusted Friends/
Family Disapprove   Family Approve

| 1 | 2 | 3 | 4 | 5 |

7. OTHER MEASUREMENT
_____   _____

| 1 | 2 | 3 | 4 | 5 |

WHAT MAKES US COMPROMISE (CHEAT)?

Sometimes we rely on others to determine our level of performance. Sometimes we get lazy and relax on standards we usually follow carefully. For example, you may lose contact with close friends, stop exercising, break a diet you are committed to, or start missing appointments for no good reason.

Do you notice that the following factors influence whether you meet your standards?

APPROVAL: Do you let the approval of others influence your standards?

FEAR: Are you afraid of failure or even success in reaching goals?

CONVENIENCE: Is it more convenient to change the standard or the level of performance?

TIME: Do you run out of time to do a good job or to even get started?

OVERWHELMING OBSTACLES: Are the barriers so high that you think your standard can never be reached?

COST: When it comes to real costs, does the sacrifice seem too great?

FATIGUE: Are you tired from work, play, stress, or handling too many details?

Which ones give you the most trouble? You can improve your personal standards of quality if you're aware of what stops you. Circle the number that indicates the degree to which each of the compromise factors affects your personal quality performance.

Approval of others

Major Barrier				No Problem
1	2	3	4	5

Fear

Major Barrier				No Problem
1	2	3	4	5

Convenience

Major Barrier				No Problem
1	2	3	4	5

Time

Major Barrier				No Problem
1	2	3	4	5

Overwhelming obstacles

Major Barrier				No Problem
1	2	3	4	5

Cost

Major Barrier				No Problem
1	2	3	4	5

Fatigue

Major Barrier				No Problem
1	2	3	4	5

THE THREE C's OF QUALITY

> *It is always with the best intentions that the worst work is done.*
>
> Oscar Wilde

The Three C's of quality—*Commitment, Competence* and *Communication*—are the intangible basics of your personal and organizational quality goals. You can't really touch or measure them, but no quality plan can succeed without them.

Commitment is the determined spirit of an Olympic swimmer who practices alone during hundreds of pre-dawn hours. *Competence* is the inner knowing of a well-trained pilot who uses all available knowledge—training, instruments, and intuition—to make quick decisions. *Communication* is the critical personal contact and mutual agreement among managers and employees that makes work flow smoothly.

As a house is built on a concrete substructure, a quality plan is built on a foundation of commitment, competence, and communication.

CORNERSTONE OF QUALITY #1

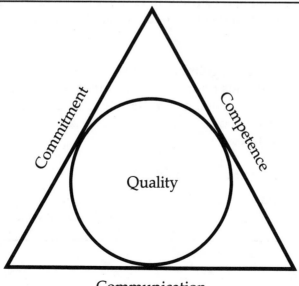

COMMITMENT

> A Harvard undergraduate who knew himself well, left this note on his door for his roommate: "Call me at seven. I absolutely have to get up at seven. Don't give up. Keep knocking until I answer." At the bottom he wrote: "Try again at nine."

Commitment is a matter of degree. It is situational as illustrated in the story above. Complete commitment to quality at work is defined as *a decisive personal or organizational choice to follow through on an agreed-upon plan of action.* Workers will be committed to quality to the extent that management is committed.

Everyone is committed to something to some degree. Our commitments vary according to their importance and our ability to meet them. For a business to succeed in its commitment to quality, every employee must be committed to quality in every detail.

EXAMPLE

Frank works as a keypunch operator typing coding sheets. He has been told, "Don't think, just type what you see." Frank knows he is typing obvious errors, such as 5 instead of a T. The programmer who receives the coding sheets corrects the errors and sends them back to Frank for retyping, a time-consuming process.

One day Frank called the programmer and asked if he would stop by his desk to look at three obvious errors and correct them so he could type them correctly the first time, thus saving correction time later. While the programmer was still at his desk, Frank asked if he saw any other obvious errors that could be corrected now.

Does Frank have a commitment to quality? Yes ☐ No ☐

To what degree would you say
he is committed? High ☐ Average ☐ Low ☐

RATE YOUR COMMITMENT

What is your level of commitment to quality in your organization? Individuals make a difference, and many individuals working as a committed whole can revolutionize the quality and productivity of your organization.

Listed below are personal and business situations that require a degree of commitment. Below them are four levels of commitment. Next to each situation put the appropriate number indicating which level of commitment you have to that item. Your answers are not right or wrong, they simply help you know yourself and where your commitment lies. Knowing yourself is the first step in making changes.

Levels of Commitment

1) Unwavering   3) Casual

2) Diligent   4) When I'm in the mood

Personal and Business Situations

____ Marriage   ____ Learning   ____ Helping others

____ Customers   ____ Personal quality standards   ____ Enjoying life

____ Family   ____ Organizational goals   ____ Doing my best work

---

COMPETENCE

Along with commitment, quality goals require actions and attitudes based on competence. Competence can be described as "know-how." Astronauts must be competent. The same is true of pharmacists, surgeons, firefighters, and payroll personnel. Each must possess certain specific measurable skills, sound education, good intuitive judgment, an ability to apply related knowledge to solve problems and a responsible attitude. Competent people and quality work go hand in hand, because competent people make sure they successfully meet agreed-upon requirements.

People who do not perform their jobs competently are generally functioning at a low level in other areas of their lives as well. Without competence, employees are just surviving, rather than building quality into a product or service. On the other hand, successful quality programs raise morale and improve competence through education, teamwork, and incentive programs.

When organizations implement quality improvements in an orderly way, they are exhibiting competence at the organizational level. They provide a master quality plan and involve all employees in its implementation. They also provide education about quality at all levels from top management down. The quality plan and the training are designed to improve competence. Improved competence will, in turn, improve quality. It also improves autonomy, teamwork, job security, and profits. Organizations help people develop competence by giving them the right tools and making them reponsible for their work.

RATE YOUR COMPETENCE

Listed below are areas of personal and professional competence. Under each topic, list those areas in which you would like to improve and those with which you are satisfied. With the help of your manager, family, or friends, begin setting new competence goals for the areas you want to improve, and pat yourself on the back for the ones you are doing well.

NEEDS IMPROVEMENT *I'M SATISFIED*

Job Skills

_____   _____
_____   _____

Education

_____   _____
_____   _____

Job Experience

_____   _____
_____   _____

Communication Skills

_____   _____
_____   _____

Solving Problems

_____   _____
_____   _____

Making Decisions

_____   _____
_____   _____

Leisure Time

_____   _____
_____   _____

Organizing

_____   _____
_____   _____

Others

_____   _____
_____   _____

COMMUNICATION

George Bernard Shaw once said, ''The problem with communication is the illusion that it is complete.'' Communication problems are the number one headache in most groups—families, companies or among friends. In spite of good intentions, people often have problems getting the message across to others effectively. Between the *sender* and *receiver* something gets lost in the translation. The weak links in communication include an *unclear purpose, garbled messages, barriers* (such as a hidden agenda, cultural differences, jargon, etc.) and little or no *feedback.* The diagram on the next page shows how quality communication works.

The purpose of communication* is to achieve mutual understanding. The definition of communication comes from the Latin word *communis* meaning, ''commonness,'' a *commonness of understanding.* A common understanding and mutual agreement cannot take place with one-way messages. Too often we send a message and assume it is received and understood the way we intended.

> An American tourist in a Madrid restaurant wanted to order steak and mushrooms. He spoke no Spanish; the waiter knew no English. The diner drew a picture of a mushroom and a cow. The waiter left the table and returned a few moments later with an umbrella and a ticket to the bullfights.

---

*For an excellent book on communication order *The Art of Communicating* by Bert Decker using the information in the back of this book.

QUALITY COMMUNICATION INFINITY MODEL

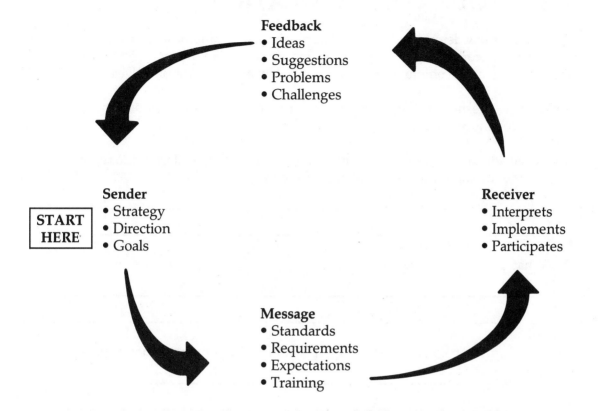

In the above model, both sides are responsible for success. For effective communications, the process is continuous until mutual understanding has been reached on the topic under discussion.

You can dramatically improve communication at home and at work if you and other key people remember these guidelines:

1. Determine the true *purpose* of your message.
2. Consider the *perception* of your audience.
3. Use the appropriate *channel* for delivery.
4. Obtain *feedback* to check for mutual understanding.
5. Continually *improve* your communication skills.
6. Take advantage of *training* opportunities.
7. *Reinforce* and *reward* good communication.

All groups have established communication systems, both formal and informal. For a quality program to work effectively, an organization must have a specific communication channel to send and receive information about the quality process.

RATE YOUR COMMUNICATION

Quality is largely determined by how effectively you communicate in your personal and work life. We communicate more effectively when we understand the expectations in communication and set usable standards for ourselves.

Answer the questions below to clarify your communication expectations and to set your communication standards.

1. When you are the sender of information, what do you need from the receiver in order to know you were understood accurately?

    _____

    _____

2. What can you do to get what you need?

    _____

    _____

3. How can you meet other peoples' expectations in a communication situation?

    _____

    _____

4. What is a reasonable standard (or goal) to set for increasing the quality and effectiveness of your present communication?

    _____

    _____

5. How will you measure your standard?

    _____

    _____

6. What are some methods of improving communication about the quality program in your organization?

    _____

    _____

When you have finished, read the authors' suggestions on the next page.

AUTHOR'S COMMENTS

1. Feedback! Feedback! Feedback! Most of us do not *give* or *get* enough feedback to complete the communication loop. Feedback is written, verbal, and nonverbal.

2. You can ask, "What is your reaction to my suggestion (or statement)?" Also, look carefully for non-verbal signals as they tell you more than words do. When writing, ask for a written response.

3. Ask them how you can help them. Listen attentively. Provide verbal and non-verbal feedback. Paraphrase. Be open-minded.

4. Same as No. 3, and KNOW YOUR PURPOSE.

5. Self-evaluation and feedback from others. Do I feel more competent as a communicator? Are my projects completed in less time with less errors and stress? Are people giving me better quality information in appropriate detail?

6. Communication (and plenty of it) is the Number One way to create quality awareness. Write the word "QUALITY" on the walls and floormats, and write about it often in your organization's newsletter. Create slogans—have a contest—and put quality statistics and improvement charts in the dining and lounge areas. Spread the word and say it with pride. Make quality an integral part of your company culture. Management should talk about quality regularly. Make it the first agenda item at department meetings.

DOUBLE YOUR COMMUNICATION

SUGGESTIONS FOR COMMUNICATING QUALITY

Start a newsletter about quality	Conduct status meetings
Make a video about quality	Organize recognition parties for quality performance
Create quality groups	Write-up policy statements (written and spoken)
Management—hold employee talk sessions	Organize pep rallies
Have suggestion boxes and forums	Talk with customers

In his book *Quality Without Tears,* Phillip Crosby tells the following story to illustrate an active approach to communicating a quality problem:

A management team was concerned about the errors in computer programming. The team members felt that these put an unusually heavy burden on the mainframe computer, since it was being used primarily for troubleshooting. They estimated a cost of $250,000 due to the problem of the software's not being close enough to specification before troubleshooting began. Rather than just telling people about this, they borrowed ten brand-new Cadillacs and lined them all up in the front yard. Then they invited everybody out to "see what troubleshooting costs us." That made a big impression.

THIS WOULDN'T HAPPEN IF HE HAD TO PAY FOR THE COST OF HIS ERRORS

YOUR ORGANIZATION'S GOALS

> *If you don't know where you're going, you will probably end up somewhere else.*
>
> Laurence J. Peter

Quality standards are based on an organization's policies and goals. Goals create unity and group identity. Employees cannot help the organization reach its goals if they don't know what they are.*

An organization's goals are usually divided into four categories:
- The corporate mission statement
- Divisional objectives
- Each department's responsibilities
- Each employee's personal work responsibilities

Goals are based on what the company wants to accomplish: solving problems, manufacturing products, or providing services. For goals to succeed, everyone must understand them and agree to them. The corporate mission must be in agreement with division, departmental, and individual work responsibilities.

EXAMPLE

XYZ Corporation manufactures warblets. The manufacturing division of XYZ is very efficient and has set a production goal of 10,000 friblets in the first quarter. One friblet is attached to each warblet. The corporate forecast calls for production of 5,000 warblets. Is the manufacturing division working effectively toward organizational goals? How could they be more efficient in working with other departments or divisions to meet the organization's goals?

There's a high cost in failing to communicate and agree on goals, because in their absence, everyone makes their own rules. In a service organization, communication breakdowns such as these may account for as much as 30-40% of operating cost.

---

*For an excellent companion book order *Motivating at Work* by Twyla Dell using the information in the back of this book.

YOUR MISSION POSITION

Can you answer the following questions about your organization and your role in it? Knowing the part you play in the functioning of your organization is an important step toward creating meaningful quality guidelines.

1. Describe your organization's mission.

2. What is your personal role in helping fulfill this mission?

3. List your division or department responsibilities as they relate to the organization's mission.

4. Write down your personal work responsibilities.

5. List the responsibilities of your employees (if applicable).

CHECK YOUR GOAL CONTROL

How does your organization rate in "goal control?" Check the following to see how well you think your organization's or department's goals are understood by its employees.

YES	NO	
☐	☐	Are your organization's goals in writing?
☐	☐	Are they written in clear, simple language?
☐	☐	Are they widely distributed and available to everyone?
☐	☐	Are they consistent with other areas in the organization?
☐	☐	Are they realistic?
☐	☐	Are they applicable to everyone?
☐	☐	Do they reflect management's respect for employees?
☐	☐	Are the people who set the goals talking about them and supporting them by example?
☐	☐	Do employees agree with the goals?
☐	☐	Is education available to support the goals?
☐	☐	Does management follow up when goals are set?
☐	☐	Do the goals set clearcut deadlines?
☐	☐	Do they prescribe upper and lower limits if applicable?
☐	☐	Are they expressed concretely, including figures?

IF IT ISN'T WRITTEN . . . IT ISN'T A GOAL!

SETTING QUALITY STANDARDS

Goals are the single most important factor in controlling quality. The more specific they are, the better results you can expect. From goals come controls. Controls are another way of saying "quality standards." When you have an agreed-upon standard of measurement, you can depend on the result.

Controls are methods of checking to see whether you are doing what you say you are going to do when you say you are going to do it. They help you determine whether a product is fit for use. The bottom line is that goals and controls must be designed to make sure you meet your customer's needs.

The following steps are usually followed to establish controls or quality standards. These steps do not have to be complicated. In fact, they should be simple, so that you will be able to implement them effectively. Check the steps you follow regularly in your company.

GOAL-SETTING CHECKLIST

YES   NO

☐ ☐   1. We have determined our corporate, division, department and personal goals.

☐ ☐   2. They are in agreement.

☐ ☐   3. We have decided what methods we will use for reaching our goals.

☐ ☐   4. We have set guidelines for acceptable work and our guidelines are standardized across the board.

☐ ☐   5. We are educating and training employees. We know our plan won't work if employees aren't informed and trained.

☐ ☐   6. We implement our work using our standards as guidelines. Our standards are incorporated into our organization's technology.

☐ ☐   7. We check the results of the work *during* the process.

☐ ☐   8. We take immediate action to correct any problem or errors.

WHAT'S WRONG WITH THIS STORY?

XYZ Manufacturing Group held a high-level organizational meeting at an exclusive country club. Organization goals were reviewed and redefined. Each division-level manager established efficient new quality standards for employees and tight controls for enforcing the standards. A quality control expert hired by the XYZ president presented the most up-to-date methods of quality control, including sophisticated formulas to plan and chart results. The new procedures were finalized and adopted. Division-level managers received mandates to present them to their employees for immediate implementation. Employees were expected to adopt the new controls quickly and completely, and would be trained in the new procedures in the next six months.

In your opinion, what is wrong with this story? (See upside down box below for explanation.)

ANSWER: If you said that the plan lacked employee input, you are correct. The secret of success in any quality program is that the people who set the standards must be the people who will be using them! True, upper-level managers will use them, but in this story they have set standards that will apply to all levels.

Most upper-level managers and engineering specialists do not know the nuts and bolts of the workplace. At one time they were involved in day-to-day production, but processes and conditions change rapidly and it is easy to lose touch with the daily reality of meeting customer requirements. Their expertise is the big picture.

Only by involving all employees in setting the standards can a company's quality program be assured of success. If managers ignore employee input, they will be overlooking their most valuable assets for deciding what goals to adopt and the standards to measure them. When employees help set standards, executives are assured that the people implementing them are committed to them.

THE STORY RETOLD

XYZ Manufacturing Group held an important yearly conference for all of its managers and supervisors at an exclusive country club. The executive committee presented a proposed agenda of revised goals and projections for the coming year, including the implementation of a tight new quality control program. Small groups discussed the goals and approved them or suggested additional revisions. Through evaluation and feedback, new and revised goals emerged with group consensus.

A quality control expert hired by the president presented the most up-to-date methods of quality control. She then conducted small group sessions to help each department adapt the procedures to its job responsibilities. The quality expert helped managers outline a procedure for presenting the plan to their employees. The plan included asking for employee input and acceptance. She also helped the managers design training programs so that their employees would be able to implement the plan.

Division-level managers planned to meet again in six weeks to hear reports from their department managers. Based on these reports, they then adjust their goals to reflect employee input. Final goals for the coming year were presented by the president at an all-company picnic in the next six weeks. Written confirmation was in everyone's mail within three days after the picnic.

QUALITY IS A TEAM EFFORT

P.S.: THE PERFECTION STANDARD

> *If you believe in unlimited quality, and act in all your business dealings with total integrity, the rest will take care of itself.*
>
> Frank Perdue

P.S. is the **Perfection Standard** that you apply to your work to achieve quality. You can also use P.S. to refer to Personal Satisfaction, because that should be the result of working to agreed-upon specifications.

What *is* the "perfect" report, the "perfect" sales call, the "perfect" widget? Quality control experts hold varying opinions about what standard should be used to determine when finished work is "perfect" enough to release to the next process or to the customer. Quality control experts use such terms as *zero defects* and *error-free,* which means that a product or service contains no errors. That is one standard.

Some quality experts believe that errors are inescapable because humans are not perfect. The **Perfection Standard** suggests that people and organizations should decide how closely they will approximate perfection in their products or services, based on their customers' needs. This **Perfection Standard** should be zero defects if possible. However, P.S. takes into account that peaches for display in a gourmet supermarket are higher quality than those selected in a food processing plant for peach cobbler.

Perfection should be thought of as a goal rather than something that can literally be achieved. A **Perfection Standard**, then is a no-nonsense written guideline to help employees perfect their services or products according to specific agreed-upon requirements. The result is a proud employee, a suitable product or service, and a satisfied customer. P.S. helps avoid the "get-by-blues."

P.S. (PERFECTION STANDARDS)

Perfection Standards make everyone's job easier. They allow people to depend on each other. When you have a P.S., you have a goal to work toward. As the Cheshire Cat said to Alice, "If you don't know where you wish to go, then any road will do." With P.S., we know which road we want and we have signposts to help us get there.

Following are 20 characteristics of useful Perfection Standards.

1. Your Perfection Standards should come as close to zero defects as is humanly possible for your product or service.

2. They should be planned and agreed upon by all affected employees, including customers when possible.

3. They should be stated clearly and completely, in writing.

4. They must satisfy your customers' requirements.

5. They must be workable and understandable.

6. No one must deviate from the standards for any reason once they are established.

7. They must be supported by upper management (or they won't work).

8. A P.S. evolves. If the P.S. is not working or becomes outdated, it should be changed.

9. New Perfection Standards should be added as needed. All affected employees must agree and sign off on the new P.S.

10. They should be written in a way that identifies for customers exactly what they can expect to receive.

11. They should reflect a "perfection" attitude.

12. They must be results oriented.

13. They should include recognition for performance.

14. They must be taken seriously.

15. They must be included in an ongoing educational program.

16. They must reflect organizational goals.

17. They must be set for *all* functions of a department or a division.

18. They should not be dependent on inspection. They should be followed regardless of inspection. They should be inspected when something goes wrong, and the source cause should be found and corrected.

19. They should be created and met with care.

20. They must be communicated effectively and continually.

PUTTING P.S. TO WORK: "JUST DO IT!"

In order to set Perfection Standards, you need a way to measure your performance. The Seven-Step Plan that follows will help you set and measure your P.S. With proper motivation, Perfection Standards are easy to establish. This plan contains no magic; all you have to do is follow it step-by-step. It's a surefire way to improve the quality of your work immediately.

Part of the P.S. Seven-Step Plan is to define your work by what you *contribute* rather than by what you *do*. In other words, how do *you* make the company better?

EXAMPLE

Mary is a training consultant in technical education. When she evaluated what she did on her job, she said at first that she provided technical training programs for employees. After a discussion with her manager, Mary broadened her definition to state that she helped to develop competent people. Stating what she contributes is a positive way of stating what she does.

I ♥

P. S.

THE SEVEN STEP PLAN:
A PREVIEW

The Seven Step Plan outlined below helps you identify your most important work responsibilities and establish specific goals for improving the quality of each task, as necessary. These steps provide a clear, consistent blueprint of your work priorities and will help you get things done.

Step 1. List your most important tasks.

Step 2. Rank your tasks by categories.

Step 3. State the end results of each task.

Step 4. List activities that achieve the end result.

Step 5. Select your measurement standards.

Step 6. Select a P-A-S Option for each task.

Step 7. List specific goals to support your P-A-S Option.

BONUS: You can also use the Seven Step Plan to teach other employees to set quality goals.

Turn to page 48 to start your Seven Step Plan.

CORNERSTONE OF QUALITY #2.

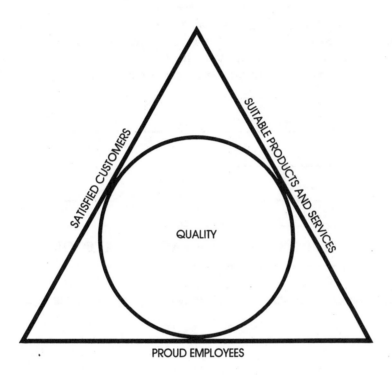

THE SEVEN-STEP PLAN FOR MEASURING QUALITY PERFORMANCE

STEP 1: LIST YOUR MOST IMPORTANT TASKS

Based on your organization's goals and your own job description, select the three most important tasks you perform at work and rank them in order of their importance. Later you can expand your list to include other tasks you want to measure. By beginning with the three most important, you avoid "paralysis by analysis."

Task 1. _____

Task 2. _____

Task 3. _____

STEP 2: RANK YOUR TASK BY CATEGORIES

Rank each task on a 1-5 scale (with 5 being the highest) for the following categories:

	Task 1	Task 2	Task 3
a. Helps meet organization goals	_____	_____	_____
b. Helps meet departmental goals	_____	_____	_____
c. Meets my job description	_____	_____	_____
d. Provides personal satisfaction	_____	_____	_____
e. Contributes to the organization	_____	_____	_____
f. Makes work smoother for co-workers	_____	_____	_____
g. Creates profit for the organization	_____	_____	_____
h. Helps put the organization in a leading position	_____	_____	_____
i. Provides long-term value	_____	_____	_____

THE SEVEN-STEP PLAN (CONTINUED)

STEP 3: STATE THE END RESULT(S) OF EACH TASK

Write down the end result of each of the three priority tasks you listed in Step 1. What does each task look like when it is complete? These completed tasks are your product or service that will meet your final expectation or the expectations of your manager or customer.

Example:

Task: *Write service orders*　　　　End result: *Service order delivered to maintenance*

Task 1. _____　　　　End result: _____

Task 2. _____　　　　End result: _____

Task 3. _____　　　　End result: _____

STEP 4: LIST ACTIVITIES THAT ACHIEVE THE END RESULT

What specific activities do you perform to achieve the end results listed above?

Example:

Task: Write service orders　　　　End result: *Deliver orders to maintenance*

Tasks performed: *Take information from customer Fill out the form*

Task 1: _____　　　　End result: _____
Tasks performed: _____

Task 2: _____　　　　End result: _____
Tasks performed: _____

Task 3: _____　　　　End result: _____
Tasks performed: _____

THE SEVEN-STEP PLAN (CONTINUED)

STEP 5: SELECT YOUR MEASUREMENT STANDARDS

From the list below determine which standards you will use to measure the three tasks. Your measurement helps you determine whether your work is satisfactory or needs improvement. Not every function of every task needs measurement.

TASK 1 I Will Measure:		TASK 2 I Will Measure:	TASK 3 I Will Measure:
☐	Quantity	☐ Q	☐ Q
☐	Quality	☐ Q	☐ Q
☐	Cost	☐ C	☐ C
☐	Time	☐ T	☐ T
☐	Accuracy	☐ A	☐ A
☐	Customer satisfaction	☐ Cs	☐ Cs
☐	Flexibility	☐ F	☐ F

STEP 6: SELECT A P-A-S OPTION FOR EACH TASK

Select your P-A-S Option below. Your P-A-S Option is the standard that is the most appropriate choice for each activity. Which option is best for your specific tasks?

PERFECTION Option: No mistakes, zero defects, inflexible

AVERAGE Option: Past results are fine, very flexible

STRETCH Option: Reasonable difficulty, little flexibility

For many tasks, average is appropriate. Your challenge will be to maintain your P-A-S Option choice. Remember, choose your options carefully and then perform them as agreed.

THE SEVEN-STEP PLAN (CONTINUED)

STEP 7: LIST GOALS TO SUPPORT YOUR P-A-S OPTIONS

In Task #1, what is your most important measurement. (Step 5)? _____

Your P-A-S Option choice (Step 6) for Task #1: _____

List three specific goals that will help you maintain your P-A-S Option choice:

1. _____

2. _____

3. _____

In Task #2, what is your most important measurement (Step 5)? _____

Your P-A-S Option choice (Step 6) for Task #2: _____

List three specific goals that will help you maintain your P-A-S Option choice:

1. _____

2. _____

3. _____

In Task #3, what is your most important measurement (Step 5)? _____

Your P-A-S Option choice (Step 6) for Task #3: _____

List three specific goals that will help you maintain your P-A-S Option choice:

1. _____

2. _____

3. _____

The goals you have set in Step 7 are your beginning steps for measuring and improving the quality of the most important tasks you perform. Each month you can add a new task, evaluate the steps, and set an improvement goal. At the same time you can re-evaluate your original goals and decide whether you want to make changes.

AN ACTION-ORIENTED QUALITY PLAN

Quality challenges will not disappear when you initiate your Seven-Step Plan, but you will have an organized method of coping with those problems. The sort of challenges that turn up are problems to be solved, opportunities, or new goals to be met. The chart below suggests another easy method for defining challenges as they occur in your work environment.

CHALLENGES	CORE TASKS	COMPLETION DATE	WHO IS RESPONSIBLE
There are no quality guide-lines for sales force.	Do Seven-Step Plan quality exercises to set three priorities for sales force.	October 15	Tom Clifton Gayle Lucci
P.S. plan for Data Processing typing pool is outdated.	Choose new P-A-S Options	September 30	Dori Bell Louise Hanson

GETTING RESULTS

Once you have adopted your Perfection Standards you must show results. When you examine the results of applying your P.S. ask yourself the following questions:

Did you receive the results you expected?

Did you receive any benefits you didn't expect? What are they?

How can your positive results be made even better?

Would you make changes based on the results? What kind?

Are there any negative results? What are they?

Can you change them? How?

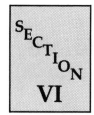

SECTION

VI

THE "HOW-TO"
OF QUALITY

> *There will be two kinds of companies in the future—companies which have implemented total quality, and companies which are out of business.*
>
> Robert Millar

This chapter addresses basic quality issues from a "how-to" point of view. In his book, *Believe and Achieve*, Sam Cypert tells this story about the legendary coach of the Green Bay Packer football team, Vince Lombardi and the basics.

Once, after the Green Bay Packers football team had played a particularly bad game, Coach Lombardi got on the bus, held up the ball, and said, "Gentlemen, this is a football." From the back of the bus, a player spoke up and said, "Coach, slow down; you're going too fast for us..."

Because quality is not an object like a football, it is harder to identify. However, we *can* identify individual components of quality. In this section we will introduce ten action-oriented components of a quality program, and give you some basic guidelines for addressing each. You will be given exercises to help you apply these principles in your own work.

These are the ten how-to components of a quality program. They are:

1. Identify and solve quality problems
2. Assure customer satisfaction
3. Measure results
4. Reward quality performance
5. Set up quality groups
6. Provide quality training
7. Assess the cost of quality
8. Establish your quality program
9. Support your quality program
10. Make quality work

1 | HOW TO IDENTIFY AND SOLVE QUALITY PROBLEMS

Quality is based on problem prevention. We can prevent a problem only when we understand the process. Perfection Standard (P.S.) is the means for preventing problems. Even if your goal is zero defects, problems will occur from time to time because the people, environment, and materials change over time. *A commitment to quality means stopping the process and fixing the problem.* The following steps will help you identify and solve quality problems.

FIND THE PROBLEM. Problems do not usually appear without some warning. Managers committed to P.S. check with their people often and in person to see how things are going. Managers and supervisors should visit each part of the workplace with a purpose in mind. In his book *A Passion for Excellence,* Tom Peters calls this (MBWA), Management By Wandering Around.

While wandering around, managers compare what they see to the P.S. They inquire about potential problems and create a supportive environment in which employees feel free to report problems. (If management has not clearly defined goals and P.S., however, workers may feel uncomfortable and be unwilling to discuss problems.) Management controls problem situations by knowing where the opportunities are for errors and by acting quickly when errors occur. They involve everyone in working together to solve the problem.

IDENTIFY PROBLEMS BY THEIR EFFECTS. Production is slowed by 20% (effect) because of a flu epidemic (problem). A customer is angry (effect) because he was put on hold for three minutes (problem). Effects indicate that something is happening in the process that does not meet P.S.

CHECK THROUGH THE EFFECTS TO THE CAUSE. Causes are the reasons for the problems. Some reasons may be obvious. Other source causes are less obvious. Like the skin of an onion, each layer is a suspected cause and you must peel away the layers to find the *source cause.* Unless source causes are found and fixed, the problem will probably reoccur.

When you have identified the source cause, communicate the problem to everyone involved and refer to your written P.S. If the P.S. is outdated or does not address the problem, it should be changed.

Effect:	20% decrease in productivity
Cause:	Flu epidemic
Source Cause:	Flu vaccination program not offered to company employees

Effect:	Angry customer
Cause:	On hold for three minutes
Source Cause:	Overloaded phone lines

IDENTIFY AND SOLVE QUALITY PROBLEMS (CONTINUED)

CORRECT THE SOURCE CAUSE. Involve everyone in finding the source cause and correcting it. Possible corrections to the problems just defined are: (1) Vaccinate all consenting employees immediately and set up a contingency plan for the next flu season. (2) Add additional telephone lines and provide extra personnel to answer phones during peak hours.

REINFORCE P.S. TO ASSURE PREVENTION IN THE FUTURE. Prevention results in quality; correction after the fact does not. Although it's difficult to prove, experts suggest a 10 to 1 payback with the preventive approach. It is not a flashy, award-filled approach that singles out heroes for successfully putting out fires. Rather it is a low-key strategy like preventive medicine, which simply maintains organizational health and quality without fanfare. The result is that costs are reduced and the mission gets accomplished.

RECHECK TO MAKE SURE THE PROBLEM HAS NOT REOCCURRED. Many problems do not disappear completely with the first solution, and it is important to periodically check to make sure quality remains in place.

ASK THESE QUESTIONS TO SOLVE A PROBLEM

PROBLEM-SOLVING CHECKLIST

Following is a checklist to help you pinpoint personal attitudes and work situations that can create problems if they are not approached with a positive attitude. Check those that apply to you and evaluate your score at the bottom of the page.

	YES	NO	
1.	☐	☐	I work actively to support management decisions regarding quality in our organization.
2.	☐	☐	I keep my ego in check and work as a team member to complete quality goals.
3.	☐	☐	I am satisfied with quality as it is and wonder what all the fuss over quality is about.
4.	☐	☐	I rely on my own experience and seldom seek the opinions of others when completing quality goals.
5.	☐	☐	I am mindful of tunnel vision and always try to see the good of the whole organization in my quality goals.
6.	☐	☐	I work enthusiastically toward my quality goals in order to keep the morale high in my department.
7.	☐	☐	I refrain from living in the past when things were simpler, and deal realistically with the more complex workplace of today.
8.	☐	☐	I seldom take advantage of the professional training in quality performance and problem solving offered by my organization.

ANSWERS: YES: 1,2,5,6,7. NO: 3,4,8. If you have these answers, you are on the quality bandwagon and are part of the solution rather than part of the problem. If you have other answers than these, check your attitude toward quality and adjust accordingly.

PROBLEM SOLVING EXERCISE

1. Choose a product or service in your department that has a recurring problem. State the problem. (Problems are deviations from standards.)

2. List the effects or consequences of the problem. (All problems reveal themselves by their effects.)

3. List the *source causes.* Be objective. Pointing the finger of blame at a person creates a smokescreen that keeps you from finding the real cause. Consult the people involved if you are uncertain about causes.

4. Determine what preventive action you can take.

5. Follow up to verify your results.

FACE the Facts

You can summarize the previous problem-solving exercise by remembering this mnemonic. It will help you to *FACE the facts* and become a world-class problem solver.

Find the facts
Analyze alternatives
Choose and implement
Evaluate the results

---

2 | HOW TO ASSURE CUSTOMER SATISFACTION

> *Quality is what the customer says it is.*
>
> Dr. Armand Feigenbaum

The first and truest test of quality is whether a product or service meets your customers' requirements. The payoff for P.S. comes from a customer's trust that a product or service has been reliable over a long period of time. Your company is assured of success when all of your products or services succeed and your customers recommend you by saying, "We have confidence in everything they sell."

Most customers are easy to please. They simply want us to do what we say we are going to do when we say we are going to do it. They are also pleased, and surprised, when we take time to follow up and ask if they are satisfied. The idea of calling is easy but its implementation is rare. Imagine how many compliments and good ideas you would receive if you viewed follow-up calls as opportunities rather than threats.

Some interesting statistics tell why companies lose customers:

1% of lost customers die.
3% move away.
4% just naturally float.
5% change on friend's recommendations.
9% can buy it cheaper somewhere else.
10% are chronic complainers.
68% go elsewhere because the people they deal with are indifferent to their needs.

Our customers are not the frosting on the cake—*they are the cake.* The frosting is an improved reputation and higher profits as a result of a quality job.

For an excellent companion book on customer satisfaction order *Quality Customer Service* by William B. Martin and/or *Customer Satisfaction: The Second Half Of Your Job* by Dru Scott using the information in the back of this book.

ENCOURAGE CUSTOMERS TO COMPLAIN

You and your customers should be friends. Aside from skilled workers, the best improvement ideas come from customers. A wise organization uses the information to improve quality and service. Several Japanese companies have been encouraging consumer feedback by including this statement in their product packaging:

"Accepting bad products without complaint is not necessarily a virtue."

Most customers don't complain. They quietly switch to another product or service. However, they would probably remain loyal if they were encouraged to complain and something was done to improve the product or service as a result.

You can encourage your customers to help you make a better product by asking them to complain. The following guidelines are helpful:

1. Make it easy for customers to complain. Use complaint forms and 800 phone numbers and check on customers personally for their feedback.

2. Listen to the complaint. Ask questions. Ask for suggestions.

3. Make sure the complaints reach the right people.

4. Act quickly and with goodwill to solve the problem.

5. Replace defective products immediately, without charge.

6. Take positive steps to prevent the problem's recurrence.

To bring the concept of quality closer to home, you can apply the same tests to your *internal* customers as to your external customers. Think of your internal customers as your personal customers, those co-workers who receive the work that you complete. Your personal customers should be treated even better than your outside customers, because *you're sure you'll be seeing them again.* The following worksheet will help you identify your personal customers and your quality goals in relation to them.

PERSONAL CUSTOMER WORKSHEET

1. My personal customers are:

2. My P.S. goal for my product or service is (Review Step 7 of your Seven Step Plan) shown on page 51.

3. Answer yes or no to the following questions:

YES NO

☐ ☐ Do I establish my P.S. with my personal customers in mind?

☐ ☐ Do I talk to my personal customers regularly?

☐ ☐ Do I ask how I'm doing for them?

☐ ☐ Do I ask my customers if they are satisfied?

☐ ☐ Do I request honest feedback or suggestions?

☐ ☐ Do I look at my product or service from a ''do unto others'' point of view?

☐ ☐ Do I correct errors and handle problems quickly and completely?

☐ ☐ Do I recheck to make sure that problems do not reoccur?

☐ ☐ Do I use my product or service myself (where applicable)?

3 | HOW TO MEASURE RESULTS

Kids count marbles, merchants count dollars and Casanovas count dates! Everything we do can be measured. In the work setting we need exact and accountable measurement systems that pinpoint performance while leaving room for intuitive measures as well. The personal standards evaluations in Chapter 2 are examples of intuitive, subjective evaluation.

The first step in measuring results is to collect information to see where you stand. This *baseline data* is used as a benchmark to see how effective future changes and efforts will be in improving performance. Lousy data leads to lousy decisions. Take the time to measure well and get the employee whose work is being measured to support the idea.

What to Measure
- Quantity (dollars, number produced, pages)
- Cost (dollars, over budget, under budget, profit, loss, breakeven)
- Time (minutes, hours, overtime, "undertime", time saved)
- Accuracy (mistakes, defects, proximity, inches, preciseness, corrections)
- Flexibility (speed in changing and adapting to new requirements)
- Customer satisfaction (compliments, complaints, increase in orders)

When to Measure
The best time to measure is when you can get the most accurate picture of what's happening. This "snapshot" should record reality without affecting the results. If the measurement affects the results, you are not recording performance, but the reaction to the measurement. Sometimes you want to do this—to use measurement as a motivator. The drawback is that it no longer records reality.

Tools for Measuring
- Observation
- Customer surveys (see sample that follows)
- Before and after measures (pre and post tests)
- Primary data that you collect
- Secondary data you get from others
- Line graphs (data points are charted over days/weeks/months and connected with a line)
- Bar graphs (cumulative data is stacked in bar form to show comparisons of total time, money, defects or hours worked)
- Control charts (line or bar graphs are used along with horizontal lines to show the upper and/or lower limits of acceptable performance)

Remember When You Measure
- Inform people about the measurement system.
- Give the reasons for measuring.
- Let people know what will happen with the results.
- Measure in a way that performance is not affected by the act of measuring.
- Measure unobtrusively without spying.

CUSTOMER QUALITY SURVEY

$$\boxed{\text{EXAMPLE}}$$

We appreciate your business and want to continue providing high-quality products and services that meet your specifications. We'd also like to do it on time. Please answer the following questions to assist us in our ongoing efforts to meet high quality standards.

RATING SCALE: 1=LOWEST SCORE, 5=HIGHEST SCORE

1. How would you rate our responsiveness to your needs?	1	2	3	4	5
2. How would you rate the delivery of the product/service?	1	2	3	4	5
3. What is the rating for our timeliness in serving you?	1	2	3	4	5
4. Are we changing with your changing needs?	1	2	3	4	5
5. How would you rate our face-to-face interaction?	1	2	3	4	5
6. How would you rate our telephone interaction?	1	2	3	4	5
7. What's the rating for our follow-up (after the sale)?	1	2	3	4	5
8. What's your overall impression of our quality?	1	2	3	4	5
9. Do our personal standards support our working relationship?	1	2	3	4	5
10. How would you rate the quality of our communication?	1	2	3	4	5

GENERAL COMMENTS:

THANK YOU FOR YOUR FEEDBACK

4 | HOW TO REWARD QUALITY PERFORMANCE

Don't you love getting things! It's nice to get tangible gifts on birthdays and Christmas or Hanukkah. It's also pleasing to receive those little intangible gifts of appreciation, compliments, or recognition. The reward system in your organization may be very formal or quite casual. What it should do is recognize and promote goal-related activities.

What to Reward
- Reward results more than effort.
- Reward efforts that directly support specific goals.
- Reward critical performance rather than routine tasks.
- Reward performance that sets good examples for others.

When to Reward
- As soon after the performance as possible.
- Reward in public rather than in private.
- When the example would improve employee performance.
- When it will reinforce your quality commitment to your customers.
- When it reinforces organizational and personal standards.

How to Reward
- Start by rewarding frequently.
- Gradually require more/better performance before rewarding.
- Be sure to reward the little things that contribute to quality.
- Be specific about what is being rewarded.
- Be as sincere as possible.
- Show your feelings and appreciation for the performance.
- Tie the good performance to profitability and customer satisfaction.

A REWARD CAN BE A FRIENDLY LETTER OR MEMO

5 HOW TO SET UP QUALITY GROUPS

> *In my opinion, the real strength of our Quality Enhancement Process is its absolute reliance on input from the people who know the problems—and how to solve them.*
>
> John Ankeny

There are a number of structures used in quality-conscious companies to support their commitment to quality. Here is an overview:

Quality Circles
If you work in a large organization you have probably heard of or participated in quality circles. These are groups of workers who voluntarily meet to learn how to improve quality and productivity and then apply these skills to organizational problems. The original idea revolved around weekly meetings that included:
- Leader and member training
- Project selection
- Data collection/verification
- Implementing solutions
- Management presentations
- New project selection

The author's experience while managing quality circles at National Semiconductor led to specific changes that gave the program quick and visible results in order to maintain the support of the organization. These included:
- Shorter projects
- Selecting only projects with a direct organizational impact.
- "Mini" management presentations for updating and reducing member anxiety.

These and other formalized changes have been tested by hundreds of groups over the past few years. A more recent development, the quality team, continues the evolution by requiring wider participation and results in a dramatic increase in the number of projects completed each year.

The Quality Council
A variation on the quality circle concept is the idea of a corporate quality council. The council is made up of members of each division of the organization. It also includes members from each level of management, supervision, and first-line employment. The group meets regularly to identify, analyze, and correct quality issues within the firm. They perform interdepartmental problem-solving functions.

SETTING UP QUALITY GROUPS (CONTINUED)

Rolestorming

Rolestorming is a combination of several group ideas using a technique developed by the authors to increase consensus building, creativity, and quality performance. The composition of the group, meeting times, and other details should be tailored to your organization's needs.

Rolestorming is part of a process called Profile-Scans™* which solicits, refines, and focuses group input in about one hour. Rolestorming asks each participant to combine roleplaying and brainstorming to expand idea-generating power in the room. It goes like this:

1. Pretend you are someone who is a stakeholder but not present at the meeting.

2. Consider their ideas, goals, problems, and concerns.

3. From their perspective, brainstorm ideas and comments about the quality issue being discussed.

The Q-Panel

A Q-panel is an educational forum featuring a group of internal and external authorities, lecturers and practitioners. In practice, it brings expert knowledge on quality issues and makes them personally available to individual employees. A variation on the Q-Panel is an Invitational meeting where individual experts or department heads are invited to speak in depth about their expertise in quality areas.

---

*Profile-Scans is a trademark of MANFIT-Management Fitness Systems.

SETTING UP QUALITY GROUPS
(CONTINUED)

ANN'S STORY

Ann is in charge of the quality program in her department. Her department is responsible for customer support for a large software development company. The department has set Perfection Standards of:

1. Answering customer calls by the third ring.
2. Treating every customer as they themselves would like to be treated.
3. Having a two-hour turnaround on all calls.

Although Ann is committed to quality, she is shy, and when she sees a problem she hesitates to interfere. Lately people in her department have gone back to their old ways of handling customer calls and the new quality goals seem to be forgotten. Which of the following should Ann do to get her department back on track?

_____ Call a quality meeting of the whole department.

_____ Ignore the problem.

_____ Talk to her manager.

_____ Continue to set a quality example.

_____ Scold employees for not meeting quality goals.

_____ Attend a Dale Carnegie course.

_____ Check with people individually to see how they are doing with their goals.

_____ Take a survey to see what the quality problems are.

_____ Set up a Q-Panel and do some rolestorming.

_____ Leave the organization.

ANSWERS: Ann should talk with her manager first. She should explain her shyness and ask for help. With her manager's support she should check with people individually to see how they are doing with their goals. A survey would also be helpful. After collecting the feedback she should call a meeting of the department and set up a Q-panel as a means of solving some of the quality issues. In the meantime, Ann should continue to set a quality example, and perhaps sign up for a seminar to increase her confidence.

SETTING UP QUALITY GROUPS (CONTINUED)

The authors' experience consulting in finance, high-technology, and government organizations, has shown why some quality groups succeed over a long period and others fail rather quickly. Here are some guidelines for creating successful groups.

Forming a Group
When starting any type of quality group, be sure to lay the initial groundwork before progressing. Include everyone by informing them about the purpose of the group, what its goals are, and what support it will need to be effective.
1. Start with volunteers who perform well.
2. Teach, train, and educate them about personal and work quality.
3. Set goals and priorities with management.
4. Expand participation to include more of the workforce.

Running a Group
1. Be/recruit an enthusiastic and quality-educated leader.
2. Gather input and ideas from the entire organization.
3. Identify specific duties and results for each member.
4. Focus efforts on critical organizational priorities.
5. Continue to expand participation.

Participating in a Group
1. Attend and participate as agreed.
2. Work with other group members and with others in the organization.
3. Speak your mind when you agree or disagree.

Selecting Projects
1. Get as much management input as you can.
2. Stick to critical organizational priorities.
3. Start with short-term projects to build confidence and skill.

Presenting to Management
1. Schedule sessions when there's something important to present.
2. Have the entire group participate.
3. Get feedback on their satisfaction with the group's current activities.
4. Ask them about changes in plans, priorities, and strategies.

When to Disband a Group
1. When organizational quality goals cease to be met.
2. When support for the group is absent.
3. As soon as you have solved all quality issues!

QUALITY GROUP CHECKLIST

The following checklist will help you plan a quality group. If you answer yes to each question you are ready to meet as a quality group and begin discussing quality problems and solutions. Three guidelines are helpful: 1) Be creative. 2) Be positive. 3) Have fun!

YES	NO	
☐	☐	Do we have management support for setting up a quality group?
☐	☐	Will management participate?
☐	☐	Have we set mutual goals and priorities with management?
☐	☐	Has everyone been informed about the need for a quality group?
☐	☐	Do we have a meeting room?
☐	☐	Have we sent memos to people inviting them to participate? (The group should be voluntary.)
☐	☐	Do we have a designated facilitator who is experienced in running a quality group?
☐	☐	Have we decided on a format for the group? (quality circle, quality council, Q-panel, other)
☐	☐	Do we know specifically what quality issues we want to discuss?
☐	☐	Do we have an agenda?
☐	☐	Has someone been designated to record the results of the meeting and send written summaries to everyone concerned?
☐	☐	Have we planned a specific time to begin and end?
☐	☐	Have we included time for discussion and breaks?
☐	☐	Have we selected a name for our group?
☐	☐	Have we gathered input and ideas from everyone involved?
☐	☐	Have we decided how we will get feedback from the group after the meeting?

6   HOW TO PROVIDE QUALITY TRAINING

> *Quality begins and ends with education.*
>
> Kaoru Ishikawa

> *The first and most important component of management is training.*
>
> Peter F. Drucker

Thomas Gilbert reinforces training in his book *Human Competence* by stating:

SUCCESSFUL MANAGEMENT EQUALS

A. Clear expectations
B. Adequate guidance for performance
C. Best possible tools
D. Generous rewards
E. Useful training

Training can focus on current skill needs or future development. Personal and work quality will project attitudes, skills, opinions, and values that have been learned over time. The best training programs recognize that old habits are hard to break. This means you'll get better success by focusing training on critical organizational needs and by taking the long-term approach. Training is a personal and a management function.

Tips on Training

1. TIE IT IN WITH ORGANIZATIONAL OBJECTIVES.

2. GET INPUT FROM MANAGEMENT AND THOSE BEING TRAINED.

3. CHECK TO SEE WHETHER THE SPECIFIC OBJECTIVES ARE BEING MET.

4. LOOK FOR ON-THE-JOB APPLICATIONS OF THE TRAINING SKILLS.

5. *NEVER* PORTRAY TRAINING AS A LUXURY.

6. NEVER *START* CUTTING COSTS BY CUTTING TRAINING.

For a useful reference on training strategies order *Training Managers to Train* by Brother Herman E. Zaccarelli, C.S.C. using the information in the back of this book.

STARTING A QUALITY TRAINING PROGRAM (Continued)

YOUR START-UP "TO DO" LIST. (Check those you plan to incorporate into your program.)

PLAN TO DO: BY DATE:

PLAN TO DO:	BY DATE:	
_____	_____	Completed needs assessment to develop objectives
_____	_____	Budget (for complete program)
_____	_____	Advisors identified and updated
_____	_____	Geographic location selected
_____	_____	Types of instructors identified
_____	_____	Instructors hired/trained
_____	_____	Course objectives double-checked
_____	_____	Materials written/prepared
_____	_____	Specific room locations selected and reserved
_____	_____	Equipment identified, ordered and tested
_____	_____	Method of evaluating results selected
_____	_____	Student selection process outlined
_____	_____	Students notified in advance (dates, locations, etc.)
_____	_____	Process to make corrections or modifications outlined

OTHER IDEAS

_____   _____

_____   _____

RATE YOUR QUALITY TRAINING PROGRAM

Answer the following questions to rate your quality training program.

1. We have an active quality training program in our organization.
   Yes _____ No _____

2. Our quality education program is solidly supported by upper management.
   Yes _____ No _____

3. Management provides the following input for our quality education program:

4. Our quality training program can be described as follows:

5. Employees provide the following input for our quality training program:

6. Our quality training program has the following strengths:

7. We can improve our quality training program in the following ways:

8. Follow-up on quality training in our organization is achieved in the following ways:

9. On-the-job applications of quality training are implemented as follows:

10. Quality education is cost effective in our organization. Yes _____ No _____

7 | HOW TO ASSESS THE COST OF QUALITY

How much does quality cost? This is a problem—you need a way to evaluate the price you pay for quality now and the price you would pay if you put a new or more rigorous quality program in place. After it is in place, you need to continually evaluate costs in order to monitor the program. Cost is an important baseline for improvement. First of all, let's define the cost of quality.

THE COST OF QUALITY IS:
What it costs to prevent and correct problems.
The combined price of conformance and nonconformance.

Philip Crosby refines this definition further, and says that quality costs fall into three areas: *prevention* costs, *appraisal* costs, and *failure* costs.

Conformance is assuring that things are done right the first time. It includes identifying requirements and specifications, communicating requirements and specifications, and using a preventive approach to do things right the first time.

Nonconformance leads to redoing things and to unmet expectations. It wastes time and materials, creates the need for heavy inspection, and costs ten times more to correct than to prevent.

You should periodically evaluate the cost of quality, both in your business and in your personal life. When too little attention is paid to prevention, the cost of problems goes up; this is one way to alert yourself to a slackening of quality controls.

Quality in Business: To assess the cost of quality at work, be sure to include the cost of:
- Activities for preventing problems from occuring
- Inspecting products or services
- Breakdowns and defects that occur *before* delivering the product/service
- Breakdowns and defects that occur *after* delivering the product/service

Personal Quality: The personal costs of quality include the time, money, and emotional energy used to learn and practice high-quality living. It also includes the lost time, goodwill, money, and opportunity when we don't. Be sure to include the costs of:
- Preventive education, or ''learn it before you need it''
- Preventive planning and strategizing
- Time taken to develop standards
- Problems caused to ourselves by not meeting standards
- Problems caused to others by not meeting standards
- Problems caused by having the wrong P.S. standards or P-A-S options

KEEP A COST DIARY

On a diary similar to the one shown below, keep track of costs you incur as a result of not meeting your quality goals. These can be personal as well as professional costs and they can be time or people related (lost time, hurt feelings) as well as dollars and cents. Also keep track of your quality gains each month, especially as you add new goals to your 7-Step Plan.

Cost Diary

Jan. Costs	Feb. Costs	March Costs
personal *professional*	*personal* *professional*	*personal* *professional*
savings based on prevention	*savings based on prevention*	*savings based on prevention*
April Costs	May Costs	June Costs
personal *professional*	*personal* *professional*	*personal* *professional*
savings based on prevention	*savings based on prevention*	*savings based on prevention*
July Costs	August Costs	Sept. Costs
personal *professional*	*personal* *professional*	*personal* *professional*
savings based on prevention	*savings based on prevention*	*savings based on prevention*
Oct. Costs	Nov. Costs	Dec. Costs
personal *professional*	*personal* *professional*	*personal* *professional*
savings based on prevention	*savings based on prevention*	*savings based on prevention*

8 | HOW TO ESTABLISH YOUR QUALITY PROGRAM

You have probably seen various quality programs in action sometime in your career. Some have failed and some have worked. Following are some guidelines for establising a program that will succeed. Use them to start a new program or adjust your current one.

Overall Plan. Every quality consultant, book, or workshop suggests that you start with a systematic plan that covers your goals and objectives for the program. A few hours spent on planning save days and months of wasted time later.

Commitment and Support. Identify the commitment and support that will be needed to keep your quality efforts supported, visible, and rewarded when there is success. Design your program before forming groups or identifying problems.

Education and Training. Bite the bullet! Your program will fail if you don't hammer out what your workforce knows and what they need to know. The difference is what the education and training programs must cover. A sporadic and superficial overview may build emotions and morale awhile, but it won't last. Line up resources at the college level, among private firms and individuals who can assist in the effort.

Tools and Materials. Course materials are a good start. Round out what you can offer employees by adding books, videotape programs, and audio-cassette packages. A mandatory system of checkouts, reviews, and accountability for the subject content *will create better quality.*

Participation and Involvement. People want to be involved. And believe it or not, they have great ideas that will work wonders. Ask them, train them, and give them the proper tools. Follow up with quick implementation of their solid ideas to start a steady stream of productivity and quality improvement.

Measurement Indicators. Select 6 to 10 indicators that will be the final success or failure test of the program. All the efforts of the quality program should point to these indicators. Use the most appropriate data collection, graphing, and display techniques to measure reality and portray it to everyone. Discuss progress, success, and failure in terms of the agreed-upon indicators.

Rewards and Incentives. Human beings will do something for only so long without getting some form of tangible or intrinsic reward. Money, recognition, responsibility, photographs, plaques, and even red ribbons can be powerful incentives. Shoot for a combination of tangibles and intangibles along with extrinsic and intrinsic rewards. People respond to coffeecake, money in the bank, and compliments in the file. Each of us wants something different based on our current needs, so this part of the plan must have variety and frequent updates. The test is whether or not the reward leads to continued good performance.

RATE YOUR QUALITY PROGRAM

Check all boxes that apply to rate your quality program:

Exists	Up-To-Date	Effective	
☐	☐	☐	Overall plan
☐	☐	☐	Commitment and support
☐	☐	☐	Education and training
☐	☐	☐	Tools and materials
☐	☐	☐	Total participation
☐	☐	☐	Measurement indicators
☐	☐	☐	Rewards and incentives

**DON'T LET OTHERS RATE
YOUR QUALITY PROGRAM FOR YOU**

9 | HOW TO SUPPORT YOUR QUALITY PROGRAM

Everyone wants to do a quality job. However, a formal quality program takes time and energy. It also requires visible and verbal dedication from everyone involved. For some people this demand seems unnecessary. In reality, for a quality program to flourish, it must have enthusiastic, ongoing support from management and employees. Each group must make noise about quality. Lots of noise! Following are two exercises, one for managers and one for employees, to suggest positive ways of showing support for your organization's quality program. When you have completed your assessments, share your lists and ask for suggestions from other people to reinforce your commitment to your quality goals.

CORNERSTONE OF QUALITY #3

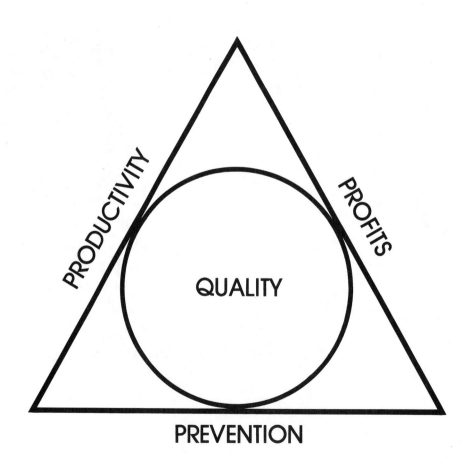

HOW MANAGEMENT AND EMPLOYEES CAN SHOW SUPPORT

1. HOW MANAGEMENT CAN SHOW SUPPORT

Some managers feel pressure because they *are* supporting quality. Others are beginning new quality programs and would like more guidelines. Still others need a shot in the arm. Listed below are eight suggestions for showing your support. Read them and check those you are already doing and any you have decided to do. In the space below, list other support actions you have taken, and those you will begin.

ALREADY WILL
DOING   DO

☐ ☐ 1. Give out pertinent quality information on strategy, goals, customers, and finances.

☐ ☐ 2. Visibly attend presentations, conferences, individual sessions, and staff meetings.

☐ ☐ 3. Solicit ideas and suggestions for changes that will benefit customers.

☐ ☐ 4. Attend training meetings.

☐ ☐ 5. Make training available to all employees.

☐ ☐ 6. Understand and support the system for measuring P.S.

☐ ☐ 7. Understand and support the reward system. (This assumes one exists!)

☐ ☐ 8. Show visible and verbal acceptance of our quality program.

Here's what else I'm doing: Here's what else I intend to do:

_____   _____

2. HOW EMPLOYEES CAN SHOW SUPPORT

Managers are often criticized for their lack of support for quality programs. They will be more effective in their efforts when they have positive support from their employees. Here are some things you can do to support your manager, the program, and your co-workers. Listed below are six suggestions for showing your support. Read them and check those you are already doing and those you have decided to do. In the space below, list other support actions you have taken, then list others you wish to begin.

ALREADY WILL
DOING   DO

☐ ☐ 1. Learn and perform all aspects of my job well.

☐ ☐ 2. Question decisions that lower quality.

☐ ☐ 3. Set good performance examples for other co-workers.

☐ ☐ 4. Establish and follow a Seven Step Plan.

☐ ☐ 5. Attend training that is offered.

☐ ☐ 6. Apply principles and techniques from training or books to the job.

Here's what else I'm doing: Here's what else I intend to do:

_____   _____

_____   _____

10 HOW TO MAKE QUALITY WORK

H igh motivation
O bjective listening
W orkable goals

T imely training
O btainable standards

M eaningful measurements
A ttention to causes
K een spirit
E rror prevention

Q uick detection
U nwavering commitment
A greement
L ifelong process
I ntegrity
T eamwork
Y es we can attitude

W ise leadership
O bservable results
R ecognition of achievement
K nowledge

A MENTION OF PREVENTION

The error that does not exist cannot be missed.

Philip Crosby

Prevention implies that problems can be resolved before they occur. In other words, an organization's goals should be to do the job right the first time. If an engineering company wants to build a bridge, they create blueprints that meet structural specifications. Imagine pouring concrete and laying beams on both sides of a river and *hoping* they will meet in the middle when the bridge is complete.

Correcting a problem after it has occurred is always more expensive and frustrating than anticipating errors and taking preventive action. The secret to preventing errors is knowing your process. Are you making semiconductors? Hamburgers? Deals? Where are the problems likely to occur? List them. Check them.

In manufacturing, this checking process is called Statistical Quality Control (SQC). Each variable of a process is identified and measured. If it moves out of control, it is readjusted. The trick is to keep all of the variables within tolerance levels. SQC shouldn't be a problem. People who make the control charts must be skilled, but people viewing them need to master only a few key items. Employees run into problems with SQC because the process isn't very exciting, and some people feel it interferes with their resourcefulness. Managers and supervisors get caught in the hero trap—unless a process is rescued at the brink of disaster, there isn't enough trouble to worry about...and no personal recognition.

For this reason, prevention isn't a particularly popular concept. It has been described as:
- Uninteresting
- Unexciting
- Unrewarding
- Unentertaining
- Uneventful

Workers don't get big gold medals for prevention, because they don't do anything visible or heroic. Managers of quality departments are seldom headliners in the company newsletter. They are the quiet people behind the scenes who are committed to slaying phantom dragons before they materialize. They are doing the silent job of making things work right and show up on schedule.

PRINCIPLES OF PREVENTION

In a well-conceived quality program, prevention is a primary focus. Even though it may be difficult to sell, it is the backbone of all successful quality programs. Prevention cuts waste, saves money, and increases productivity. Following is a list describing principles of prevention. Put a ''T'' for true next to those you think are true, and an ''F'' next to those you think are false. See the answers at the end of the list.

True or False

_____ 1. Prevention means doing the job right the first time.

_____ 2. Quality is best insured through inspection.

_____ 3. A positive attitude, communication and teamwork are all vital elements of prevention.

_____ 4. The simpler the plan or design, the less chance for error.

_____ 5. Prevention is solely the responsibility of the Chief Inspection Engineer.

_____ 6. People improve their ''prevention attention'' with incentives and training.

_____ 7. Written requirements eliminate the need for prevention.

_____ 8. Mistakes happen because people don't place importance on prevention.

_____ 9. Prevention is easier when you understand your job completely.

_____ 10. Prevention is more important in manufacturing than in a service business.

ANSWERS: 1. T; 2. F (Quality is best insured through prevention. Inspection is expensive and creates a watchdog attitude.) **3—4. T; 5. F** (Prevention is everyone's responsibility. The more people involved, the more likely that problems will be discovered quickly.) **6. T; 7. F** (Written requirements help you understand the process and goals; they do not eliminate problems.) **8—9. T; 10. F** (Prevention is equally important in both areas, but approaches to prevention may differ.)

HOW TO PREVENT ERRORS

Prevention is based on the following:

1. Clearly understanding the requirements.

2. Taking the requirements seriously.

3. Vigilance.

4. Understanding all the functions of your job or process *intimately*.

5. Doing your job right the first time.

6. Working toward continual improvement.

7. Common sense. (It is still in style.)

The young accountant in the following story could take heed of the principles listed above.

Scott is a new accountant in a large Chicago accounting firm. He became frustrated when his columns of numbers would not total correctly. Finally, in desperation, he added this line to the bottom of his data sheet: ESP $112.18. When his manager asked what the ESP meant, Scott reluctantly explained, ''Error Some Place.''

The true cost of defective work or mediocre service is almost impossible to measure. It will always be less costly to prevent mistakes than to scramble, scrap, and straighten, because scrambling occurs after the fact. Quality is not achieved through inspection and testing only—these are expensive, time-consuming methods. Reality and common sense still indicate that the best system for insuring consistent quality is to steadfastly promote prevention as a clear priority.

"Close enough" counts only in
Horseshoes
Jazz
Hand grenades
Ballroom dancing

PREVENTION VS. CORRECTION

"The 10-1 Payoff"

PREVENTION IS. . .spending time to record a message completely and fully so that you or someone else can respond properly.

While **CORRECTION IS** spending ten (10) times as many *minutes* to decipher, call back and double check for the meaning of the original message.

PREVENTION IS. . .stopping the car and looking at a map to get an accurate and direct route to a downtown address.

While **CORRECTION IS** spending ten (10) times as much *gas* driving down one-way streets, getting tickets and scaring pedestrians.

PREVENTION IS. . .providing good training and describing broad department goals so that every employee can see exactly how their work fits in and contributes.

While **CORRECTION IS** spending ten (10) times as many *hours* reprimanding, re-training, and doing the work yourself.

PREVENTION IS. . .spending one month learning the correct way to install and operate the office personal computer for word processing, database management and spreadsheets.

While **CORRECTION IS** spending ten (10) times as many *months* re-installing software, losing data and going back to the "old" way of doing things.

PREVENTION IS. . .asking the right questions and spending the time to dig out the "root" of the morale problems once and for all.

While **CORRECTION IS** spending ten (10) times as many *hours/dollars* trying half-baked solutions that deepen the feelings of mistrust and frustration.

SECTION VIII

QUALITY BEGINNING TO END: A REVIEW

Section I   **Quality Consciousness**
* Quality is a goal or a set of requirements.
* Quality consciousness is the first step in implementing a personal or organizational quality plan.
* "No worse than anyone else" is not a quality philosophy.
* Quality standards have many advantages and few disadvantages.

Section II   **Personal Quality Standards**
* Personal quality standards control our actions and decisions all day, every day.
* Setting goals improves personal quality standards.
* Individuals make hundreds of quality decisions every day.
* Anytime you expect products, services or activities to meet certain standards use your Q - M-A-T-Ch (Meets Agreed Terms and Changes) to assess your results.
* Quality is meeting expectations. Set useful workable standards with your P-A-S Options. Use Perfect, Average or Stretch depending on your goals.
* We compromise our quality standards for the following reasons: need for approval, fear of failure (or success), convenience, time, overwhelming obstacles and fatigue.

Section III   **The Three C's of Quality**
* Commitment, competence and communication are the cornerstones of quality.
* Commitment is a decisive personal or organizational choice to *follow through* on an agreed-upon plan of action.
* Competence is "know-how". Improved competence through experience and education improves quality.
* Communication is a common understanding among individuals and groups. Breakdowns occur when purposes are unclear.
* Commitment, competence and communication should be acknowledged and rewarded.

Section IV   **Your Organization's Goals**
* Quality standards are based on your organization's written policies and goals.
* Goals help organizations determine what they do: solve problems, manufacture products, provide services.
* If quality goals are set from the top they must be agreed upon at all levels.
* Organizational agreement, education and management support insure successful goal control.

QUALITY BEGINNING TO END: A REVIEW (Continued)

Section V **P.S.: The Perfection Standards**
* Perfection Standards (P.S.) depend on the need for perfect products or services.
* P.S. is based on results oriented attitudes.
* If perfection is not necessary, it should not be the goal.
* Use the Seven Step Plan to measure your performance and quality goals for your work tasks (See page 46).
* Your P.S. is successful if you can show results.

Section VI **The ''How-To'' of Quality**
* These ten basic components of quality are helpful in beginning or changing a quality program:
  1. Identify and solve quality problems. A commitment to quality means stopping the process and fixing the problem.
  2. Assure customer satisfaction. Quality is what the customer says it is. Respect your customers and encourage their feedback.
  3. Measure results. Constantly collect data to see where you stand.
  4. Reward quality performance. Formal and informal rewards keep the romance in a quality program.
  5. Set up quality performance. Quality circles, quality councils, quality panels, and rolestorming sessions provide group support and pinpoint quality problems.
  6. Provide quality training. Education is the beginning and end of all quality programs.
  7. Assess the cost of quality. Costs are prevention costs, appraisal costs, and failure costs. Costs go up as prevention goes down.
  8. Establish your quality program. To establish a quality program you need a plan, commitment, education, tools, participation, support, measurement and rewards.
  9. Support your quality program. Quality programs take time, energy and support from both management and employees.
  10. How to make quality work from motivation and training, to attitude and leadership, it all spelling quality and success.

Section VII **A Mention of Prevention**
* Prevention implies that problems can be resolved by anticipating them before they occur.
* Correcting problems after they occur is more expensive than anticipating errors and taking preventive action.
* To prevent errors, know your process or service.
* Prevention is unpopular because it is uninteresting.
* Common sense promotes prevention.
* Prevention vs. correction is a 10-1 payoff.

GLOSSARY

Acceptable Quality Level (AQL)- Pre-determined levels of defects that will be accepted.

Appraisal- The inspection of the results of performance (product, service or activity) after it has been started or completed.

Baseline Data- Performance measurement taken before trying a new method or technique.

Commitment- The motivation and desire to continue acting on beliefs, opinions and responsibilities.

Communication- The process of sending a message through selected channels to a receiver and then getting feedback to check for mutual understanding.

Competence- The self-assurance of knowing how to do something well. It is based on education and experience.

Conformance to Specification- Formal definition for quality.

Corrective Action- The process of correcting problems when the preventive approach is not used or does not work. This is the most expensive way to remedy problem situations.

Cost of Conformance- Cost of assuring that things are done right. Includes prevention and appraisal.

Cost of Non-Conformance- The cost of doing things wrong. Includes internal and external failures.

Cost of Quality- Cost of conformance + cost of non-conformance.

Customers- Those inside and outside an organization who depend on the output of your efforts. They receive the work that you complete.

Error Cause Removal (ECR)- A program where employees list problems interfering with good quality performance. Management then assigns the appropriate group or person to fix the problem.

Failure- Internal failures are problems (nonconformance) found before going to the customer. External failures are found at the client's location or in the field.

Goals- Specific milestones or objectives that you, your department or your organization wish to accomplish.

Management- Getting results through people by planning, organizing, directing, staffing and controlling.

Measurement- A record of past performance used to influence future performance. Usually in the form of quantity, quality, cost, time or accuracy.

Nonconformance- Not meeting the specified requirements.

Organizational Goals- Stated, written or implied levels of accomplishment by groups of people with common aims.

GLOSSARY (CONTINUED)

P-A-S Options- Three levels of standards (Perfection, Average, Stretch) used to gear performance to the appropriate level of customer expectations.

Perfection Standards- (7 Step Program) Measures used to see if performance matches customer requirements.

Personal Quality Standards- Quality measures for personal life based on values, opinions, and individual goals.

Planning- Outlining necessary requirements beforehand for the accomplishment of goals. Part of the preventive approach to quality.

PONC- Price of non-conformance. What it costs when you don't meet customer expectations.

Prevention- Anticipating and eliminating potential errors before they occur.

Preventive Approach- Avoiding problems before they occur leads to better products and services at lower costs.

Productivity- The ratio between *inputs* (labor, time, capital, energy) and the end product or outputs (widgets, services, completed product). Productivity can be increased either by reducing the input or increasing the output.

Q-MATCH- The acid test for professional and personal quality. *Quality = Meets Agreed Terms and CHanges.*

Quality- Conformance to specifications or requirements. Quality *does not* mean the ''goodness'' of a product, your job, or a service.

Quality Awareness- The general awareness of quality principles and their effects on the organization.

Quality Control- The process of ensuring the conformance to the designated requirements of a product or service. Often referred to as a department.

Quality Education- Knowledge, skills and practice aimed at preventing, recognizing and correcting poor quality performance.

Quality Groups- Usually made of teams of 6-12 people from an organization who study and apply quality improvement principles to work problems.

Requirements- All attributes, utilities, features and benefits the customer expects to receive with the product or service. Your customer may be your boss, a co-worker or another department.

Rework- Doing something at least one extra time due to nonconformance to requirements.

Statistical Quality Control- The use of statistical techniques for active control during the process. Makes use of real-time data for decision making. Also called statistical process control (SPC).

Trend Chart- Historical data shown in a graphical format. Usually in the form of line or bar graphs.

Zero Defects- The idea that perfection is the goal and no defects should be tolerated.

BIBLIOGRAPHY

Quality is Free
The Art of Making Quality Certain
Philip B. Crosby, 1979
McGraw-Hill Book Company, New York

Quality Without Tears
The Art of Hassle-Free Management
Philip B. Crosby, 1984
McGraw-Hill Book Company, New York

A Passion For Excellence
Tom Peters, 1985
Random House, New York

The Improvement Process
How America's Leading Companies Improve Quality
H. James Harrington, 1987
McGraw-Hill Book Company, New York

Total Quality Control
Engineering and Management
Armand V. Feigenbaum, 1983
McGraw-Hill Book Company, New York

Training Managers To Train
A Practical Guide to Improving Employee Performance
Herman E. Zaccarelli, 1988
Crisp Publications, Menlo Park, CA

Professional Balance
The Careerstyle Approach to Balanced Achievement
Rick Griggs, 1989
MANFIT Publications, Mountain View, CA

What Is Total Quality Control?
The Japanese Way
Kaoru Ishikawa, 1987
Prentice-Hall, Englewood Cliffs, New Jersey

Quality Control Handbook
J.M. Juran, 1979
McGraw-Hill Book Company, New York

MAY WE HEAR FROM YOU

Your feedback is important to us. We (Rick Griggs and Diana Bonet) are consultants teaching quality seminars. You can help us improve our seminars and publications and provide added value for our clients. Please take a minute to list what was most helpful for you and what could be improved in this book. Thank you for your help. Please make a copy of this page, fill it out and return it to us.

Most helpful:

Could be improved:

❏ Would like information regarding quality seminars.

Name/Company _____

Address _____

Phone _____

Please send to: Diana Bonet, Rick Griggs
                  Quality at Work
                  c/o Crisp Learning
                  1200 Hamilton Court
                  Menlo Park, CA 94025

NOTES

NOTES

NOTES

NOTES

NOTES

NOTES

Now Available From

CRISP. Learning™

Books•Videos•CD-ROMs•Computer-Based Training Products

Subject Areas Include:

Management
Human Resources
Communication Skills
Personal Development
Marketing/Sales
Organizational Development
Customer Service/Quality
Computer Skills
Small Business and Entrepreneurship
Adult Literacy and Learning
Life Planning and Retirement

CRISP WORLDWIDE DISTRIBUTION

English language books are distributed worldwide. Major international distributors include:

ASIA/PACIFIC

Australia/New Zealand: In Learning, PO Box 1051, Springwood QLD, Brisbane, Australia 4127   Tel: 61-7-3-841-2286, Facsimile: 61-7-3-841-1580
ATTN: Messrs. Richard/Robert Gordon

Malaysia, Philippines, Singapore: Epsys Pte Ltd., 540 Sims Ave #04-01, Sims Avenue Centre, 387603, Singapore   Tel: 65-747-1964, Facsimile: 65-747-0162 ATTN: Mr. Jack Chin

Hong Kong/Mainland China: Crisp Learning Solutions, 18/F Honest Motors Building 9-11 Leighton Rd., Causeway Bay, Hong Kong   Tel: 852-2915-7119,
Facsimile: 852-2865-2815 ATTN: Ms. Grace Lee

Japan: Phoenix Associates, Believe Mita Bldg., 8th Floor 3-43-16 Shiba, Minato-ku, Tokyo 105-0014, Japan   Tel: 81-3-5427-6231, Facsimile: 81-3-5427-6232
ATTN: Mr. Peter Owans

CANADA

Crisp Learning Canada, 60 Briarwood Avenue, Mississauga, ON L5G 3N6 Canada
Tel: 905-274-5678, Facsimile: 905-278-2801
ATTN: Mr. Steve Connolly

EUROPEAN UNION

England: Flex Learning Media, Ltd., 9-15 Hitchin Street,
Baldock, Hertfordshire, SG7 6AL, England
Tel: 44-1-46-289-6000, Facsimile: 44-1-46-289-2417   ATTN: Mr. David Willetts

INDIA

Multi-Media HRD, Pvt. Ltd., National House, Floor 1
6 Tulloch Road, Appolo Bunder, Bombay, India 400-039
Tel: 91-22-204-2281, Facsimile: 91-22-283-6478
ATTN: Messrs. Ajay Aggarwal/ C.L. Aggarwal

SOUTH AMERICA

Mexico: Grupo Editorial Iberoamerica, Nebraska 199, Col. Napoles, 03810 Mexico, D.F.
Tel: 525-523-0994, Facsimile: 525-543-1173   ATTN: Señor Nicholas Grepe

SOUTH AFRICA

Bookstores: Alternative Books, PO Box 1345, Ferndale 2160, South Africa
Tel: 27-11-792-7730, Facsimile: 27-11-792-7787   ATTN: Mr. Vernon de Haas

Corporate: Learning Resources, P.O. Box 2806, Parklands, Johannesburg 2121, South Africa, Tel: 27-21-531-2923, Facsimile: 27-21-531-2944 ATTN: Mr. Ricky Robinson

MIDDLE EAST

Edutech Middle East, L.L.C., PO Box 52334, Dubai U.A.E.
Tel: 971-4-359-1222, Facsimile: 971-4-359-6500   ATTN: Mr. A.S.F. Karim